R U Listenin'?

of related interest

Working with Anger and Young People
Nick Luxmoore
ISBN 978 1 84310 466 7

Helping Adolescents and Adults to Build Self-Esteem
A Photocopiable Resource Book
Deborah Plummer
ISBN 978 1 84310 185 7

Working with Gangs and Young People
A Toolkit for Resolving Group Conflict
Jessie Feinstein and Nia Imani Kuumba
ISBN 978 1 84310 447 6

Developing the Craft of Mediation
Reflections on Theory and Practice
Marian Roberts
ISBN 978 1 84310 323 3

Conduct Disorder and Behavioural Parent Training
Research and Practice
Dermot O'Reilly
ISBN 978 1 84310 163 5

Understanding Street Drugs
A Handbook of Substance Misuse for Parents, Teachers
and Other Professionals 2nd edition
David Emmett and Graeme Nice
ISBN 978 1 84310 351 6

Restorative Justice
How it Works
Marian Liebmann
ISBN 978 1 84310 074 4

Constructive Work with Offenders
Edited by Kevin Gorman, Marilyn Gregory, Michelle Hayles
and Nigel Parton
ISBN 978 1 84310 345 5

R U Listenin'?

Helping Defiant Men to Recognize
their True Potential

Terry Bianchini

Jessica Kingsley Publishers
London and Philadelphia

First published in 2008
by Jessica Kingsley Publishers
116 Pentonville Road
London N1 9JB, UK
and
400 Market Street, Suite 400
Philadelphia, PA 19106, USA

www.jkp.com

Library of Congress Cataloging in Publication Data
A CIP catalog record for this book is available from the Library of Congress

British Library Cataloguing in Publication Data
A CIP catalogue record for this book is available from the British Library

ISBN 978 1 84310 616 6

Printed and bound in Great Britain by
Athenaeum Press, Gateshead, Tyne and Wear

I had to put an angel to bed, but first felt the need to read him a story. The story would offer an insight into the work I have been involved in for the past twenty years, and some advice and guidance I believe we can all benefit from. That story has grown into this book.

Dedicated to Jack and his angelic friends
AS PROMISED

Love Mum and Dad

Acknowledgements

I would like to take this opportunity to thank my beautiful wife Adua and daughter Ann-Lucia for their love and support while writing this book. Also, to friends and family for reading various drafts of chapters and offering me constructive feedback.

Special thanks to Nick Luxmoore for his generous foreword, Dave Jones for his ceaseless encouragement and the artwork, Sandra Hemming for believing in my book and making my illegible grammar legible. And Jacquelyn Ogden, who never tired of reading numerous drafts, sat patiently listening to my ideas and anecdotes and, occasionally, passing comments that were usually criticisms but always invaluable.

Contents

Contents

Foreword

This book is about more than prisons and prisoners. It's about understanding human beings who are stuck and about helping them to unstick themselves. As such, it's implicitly a book about people in many settings – schools, pupil referral units, youth work and social work. It describes the way 'prison' is never just a place with padlocks and high walls; it's also a place in our heads. It describes how, in many ways, we become our own jailers, enforcing and re-enforcing self-inflicted 'sentences'. By understanding these metaphors, 'prison' can become a learning opportunity for everyone, provided they're 'listenin'.

Terry Bianchini describes what prison life is like. He does so with compassion and humanity but never condones crime or apologizes for people in prison whose early, formative experiences in life may well have been appalling. He doesn't believe in complaining or wasting time because he believes that everyone has the capacity to turn their lives around. By itself, this would be no more than a laudable belief but Bianchini describes how it can be done, practically. He may be compassionate and humane but he's also a hard-nosed pragmatist.

His book isn't necessarily about stopping 'defiant men' from being defiant. Defiance, stubbornness and anger may well be ways in which a man keeps himself safe, defending himself against a world he perceives as hostile. The problem is that these defences, often learned early in life, become habitual and persist even after the original danger has passed. They become the only ways in which a person can relate to other people. The challenge for professionals, friends and families is never to strip away a person's hard-won defences but to notice them, understand them, question them and help to temper them so that new responses to the world can develop alongside the old ones.

But this involves trusting people who say they want to help and trusting people can be dangerous. From the very beginning of our lives, even as we lie curled up in a balmy, harmonious womb, a promise is implicitly made to us; a promise that we'll be loved and kept safe in this lovely world. We're born and our parents are quick to make this promise explicit, 'I'll always be here for you,' they say. 'I'll always love you. I'll do anything for you.'

For many sons and daughters these promises are quickly broken – broken cruelly and broken repeatedly. And people react to broken promises and betrayal in the same way that they react to other losses, becoming wary of people, plotting revenge and resolving never to trust promises again. Defiance, stubbornness and anger become ways of expressing underlying hurt and disappointment.

Prison makes a practical kind of promise. It promises secure boundaries and a reliable, safe regime. This limited promise is attractive for some people. To trust another kind of promise, an emotional promise, a promise of respect, kindness and love between human beings is much harder.

So working with prisoners and with people who are emotionally imprisoned isn't for dilettantes and promise-breakers. Bianchini tells a story in this book about wanting to abandon a messed-up teaching session but, at the same time, not wanting to let the prisoners down because then they'd be sent back to their cells for the rest of the day, disappointed yet again. The experience of professionals not breaking promises allows people slowly to trust again, suggesting that the world isn't necessarily out to get them and that they don't therefore have to get their retaliation in first. This remarkable book describes a promise made by one professional with integrity who persists, listens, doesn't give up and remains utterly reliable – a promise kept to people who have learned never to trust promises, a promise that things can be different. Terry Bianchini begins by dedicating this book to his loved ones as promised.

Nick Luxmoore

Preface

As a child I was told that men do not cry. Having worked in prisons and the community for the past 20 years, I have heard many men cry for a variety of reasons: the length of sentence they have received, the loss of a loved one, despair of the life they lead, loneliness, frustration or anger. Every time the cry sounded the same.

It was never my intention to write a book about prison procedures or identify specific individuals who have served prison sentences. For this reason, throughout this book I have changed the names of the people I have worked with and not identified the prisons I have worked in.

It was however, my intention to write an honest book that would reflect my observations of prisons and the people who frequent them, detailing the comparisons I observed between the physical incarceration of an individual and the mental state of incarceration we can all place ourselves in and, most importantly, what we can learn from these observations to improve our quality of life.

Some Prisons are Built – Others are Created

A day in the life of a personal adviser

I unlocked the outer wooden door and then the inner iron gate that leads to the prison wing. I then turned around and locked the door and gate. The smell of communal eating at the long tables and disinfectant on the floor greeted me. Breakfast had just finished and everyone was on 'bang up' (locked in their cell) waiting for their daily routine to begin. The wing was quiet as I browsed through my notes. I was looking at the university responses I had received for a prisoner I had been working with for the past few months.

As a personal adviser, I work with people whose self-esteem has taken a beating for a variety of reasons: a prison sentence, a lost job or simply life not going to plan. I have been involved in this type of work for the past 20 years, working with people from a variety of backgrounds both in and out of prison.

The person I had come to see was Paul, an entrepreneur who had set himself up in Holland trafficking drugs. He had quite a lucrative business until he was lured back to England by a police sting (an organized police operation to apprehend a specific person or persons), where he was arrested and sentenced for five years. Paul, like a lot of people I have met in prison, made you wonder why he had decided to lead a life of crime. Why had he chosen a life that required victims for him to profit from? Ultimately, how much of a victim was he in his world of deceit? Paul had applied himself to changing his ways and recognizing his true potential. He had achieved good 'A' level grades and was now looking for advice on university placements. All reports identified an individual who was keen to take a second chance in life and make a real go of it.

I had done some research into potential courses and the universities were all keen to offer interviews. I had put a programme together to cover the next few weeks. We would run through some personal development activities, polish up on interview techniques, clarify living accommodation arrangements and benefits, attend interviews and then select the university we considered most appropriate.

As I browsed through my notes I heard a familiar shout 'R U listenin'?' This is used when a prisoner wants to catch someone's attention, whether that be another prisoner, an officer or a civilian member of staff. They have no idea if the other person is listening from the other side of their iron door or window, hence the common call 'R U listenin'?' I approached the heavy iron cell door, pulled back the oblong spy-flap and informed the prisoner that I was listening. He asked me if I knew anything about teeth. I did not. I queried his question and he told me he did not like the prison dentist and his tooth hurt like hell. I asked how long he had been in pain. 'A few months,' he replied. I then asked why he had not had his tooth looked at before. He explained that he had only been in prison for one week. When he was 'on the out', (the out meaning free, 'on the road' is another common expression for not being in prison) he had too many distractions to notice how much his tooth hurt. Now, locked up, staring at four walls for the best part of the day, he thought of nothing else but his tooth and the pain.

I realized that for me, this summed up the difference between prison life and life on the 'out'. Prison life gives you time to think. You think of what could have been, and how, given a second chance, you would not make the same mistake again, and how life is going to be so much better next time you get out. You realize that you now have the time to take a long serious look at your life and make those changes if you decide to do so, or alternatively, you can carry on down the same avenue that has a tendency to lead you back to a prison cell.

The book begins

I then thought about the people I advise outside prison: people who have jobs, families and friends, people who have the same opportunities to change but somehow have too many distractions to stop and assess their lives and realize. Many are institutionalized in the sense that they lead lives they did not choose but which were imposed upon them. They lack the knowledge and discipline to break free and recognize their true potential. I realized the prisoner had a structured environment to support him, to rehabilitate and prepare him for his release, while the people I advised outside had nothing.

Locked in their own prisons, unaware of their crime, length of sentence and ultimately their release date, I thought about the number of times I have heard the expression 'I feel trapped in my current situation'. I realized the advice and structure offered in prison is disciplined and focused on the individual's needs. This philosophy could be translated to people on the 'out'. I began analysing all aspects of prison life, from the segregation unit to the canteen. I became aware that this environment gave discipline to all aspects of life needed for a healthy well-being: physical education, healthy eating, social interaction and cognitive behaviour. I realized I had the format and material for a book I needed to write.

I believe this book not only offers insight into prison life, but also suggests ways (based on a prison model), that people can develop their self-esteem for a fuller life. I am not suggesting people contemplate a life of crime, but ask themselves the question are they guilty of not enjoying their current life to the full?

Whether they are an inmate in one of Her Majesty's prisons or one of their own making, or both, do they feel trapped in a life not of their own choosing? Do they feel unable to move forward? Do they dwell on past memories, some good, some bad? Are they like the prisoner who blames the police officer, the judge or the 'screw' (prison officer) for putting them in prison instead of accepting responsibility for their own actions? Are they guilty of believing their life would be happier if they had more money, a different job, better qualifications, were six inches taller, had blonde hair, more friends or better parents? If so, welcome to the human race, we all have these feelings at some point in our lives. However, waiting for a miracle to change our life is not the answer. A person would not wait for a bus or train or aeroplane if they knew it had been cancelled, so why wait for a miracle you know will never happen? Waiting is an excuse to dwell on the past, criticize the present and fear the future. I believe this book will offer the insight people need to appreciate what they can and cannot change. This, in turn, will give them the ability to correct past mistakes, enjoy the present and plan for the future.

Using the book

I have made a conscious effort to write a book that everyone can access regardless of their age, gender or professional interest. As it evolved, however, I realized it could be a useful tool kit for people working in the field of personal development – whether social or professional.

For facilitators, I have used icons to divide each chapter into specific chunks of work that can be seen as individual lesson plans. The icons will allow you to identify at a glance specific areas of development that you may wish to address with your learners. My recommendation is that you follow the sequence of icons as they appear in the chapter.

There is no specific timeline for delivery. The important thing is to allow the learners time to digest the information and express how their new insight could enhance their lives. This should be done by a review at the end of each session.

Assuming you have now purchased the book, it is my hope that as a facilitator you will adapt it to your specific learners. And take it to new levels.

How will you know if the book is helping your learners? Simple. If you are enjoying the session then you can usually guarantee your learners are benefiting from it. Remember, people are always quick to feed back negative experiences; you may have to prod your learners for positive feedback. All comments are good comments, provided you use the information to develop your delivery.

My advice to the individual reading the book for personal development is to read each chapter a couple of times, letting it sink in. Allow yourself time to contemplate what you have read. How will you know if you are benefiting from the book? Again it is simple. If you keep reading the book, you are probably engaging with its message. Ultimately, you and others around you should notice a difference in your levels of contentment, as you understand more about your behaviour and the behaviour of others in given situations.

Key to icons

The icons divide the chapters into bite-size chunks for delivery by the facilitator and digestible chunks for the individual reader.

 The writer. An experience from the writer used to catch the imagination and to introduce the facilitator and learners to the contents of the chapter.

 Exercises for learners and the individual. All have been tried and tested over many years and come with the writer's recommendation. I will suggest certain exercises for specific chapters but, as I have previously mentioned, nothing in this book is written in stone, therefore use the exercises as you consider appropriate.

 Factual information. Relevant to the subject being discussed in the chapter.

Case study. Ask your learners to break the case study down into smaller issues. (Spidergrams are good for doing this.) The idea is to help learners realize they may not have one big issue but lots of minor issues that are better dealt with in small chunks. The case study also shows how these issues can be resolved.

 Developing ideas. This information could be used as a way of encouraging a piece of creative writing, poetry or art.

 Let's talk. Ask your learners to try to identify and jot down any aspect of the passage they feel they are able to relate to. Ask them to share their findings with the group. This should make for an honest and comforting experience as they realize others have similar concerns.

 Re-cap. Bullet points used to support the chapter. Write them on pieces of paper and pin them around the room as subliminal affirmations.

Each chapter offers insight into a specific area of life that has a direct impact on our well-being, (i.e. our belief systems, basic needs, decision-making, self-discipline and physical health).

Concentrating on a specific area of development and encouraging people to identify obstacles to a life of contentment can sometimes be uncomfortable. Ultimately, a greater understanding by the individual and others around them will be worth any discomfort encountered.

Overview of the book
Chapter 1: Prison Life
This looks at the philosophy behind the book, exploring the concept that some people are locked inside their own personal prison.

Chapter 2: An Accessory to the Crime
Are people accessories to the crime of self-harm? Do they knowingly or unknowingly damage their well-being by the negative attitude they have towards themselves?

Chapter 3: Believing your Way Out from Within
Belief is a wonderful attribute, unless your beliefs are negative and damage your well-being. We explore the power of belief and how we can believe in our own ability to lead a contented lifestyle.

Chapter 4: Knowing your Sentence

If an individual considers their life to be a prison sentence, where did their sentence come from? Why do they feel they are imprisoned in their life? Did they give themselves the sentence or did someone else pass judgement on them?

Chapter 5: Natural Instincts

How much of the individual's behaviour can they attribute to their inherent survival instincts? We explore genetic make-up and the needs it presents us with.

Chapter 6: Offending Behaviour

We all have needs but what are they? This chapter will explain needs and why we are driven to fulfil them.

Chapter 7: Segregation

Possibly the loneliest place a prisoner can be sent, and yet many people outside the prison environment send themselves to similar places. Why they do it, how to handle it and the positive learning experience derived from it are explored.

Chapter 8: Institutionalization

What is institutionalization? Why would anyone choose it as a way of life and how can they break free from the constraints it places upon them?

Chapter 9: Rehabilitation

For a smooth transition from a life of captivity to one of freedom we need to identify negative traits and address them.

Chapter 10: Know your Jailers

In a prison, a prisoner will have a jailer who will make the majority of decisions for them. Outside prison do we have a jailer? If the answer is yes – why? Who is it?

Chapter 11: The Gym

Physical fitness has a greater impact on our well-being than many people appreciate or want to acknowledge. We look at appreciating the benefits and the need to take responsibility for it.

Chapter 12: Kitchens

Healthy eating can improve your lifestyle tenfold, so why are the majority of people ignorant of the benefits a healthy diet has upon their mental well-being?

Chapter 13: Freedom

An analysis of all the chapters that attempts to identify the common denominator that will offer the possible answer to achieving contentment.

Chapter 14: Sentence Planning

Is life a sentence? If we believe it is, we may need to structure our sentence in order for us to take control and start enjoying it.

Chapter 15: Exercise Regime

This includes exercises, linked to specific chapters for facilitators or the individual to use.

We can change our beliefs about our ability to lead a life of contentment. I will stress throughout this book that although the answers are simple, practice is difficult. I can show you how to play a violin in one hour. It may take five years of practice before you can give a solo performance. This does not mean you will not feel any benefit for five years. You will experience gratification immediately and the more you practise the better you will become. However, you must *want* to learn otherwise practising will be too difficult and you may never learn.

Throughout the book, prisoner case studies have been used as examples of my work. The reason for this is my belief that if a person in one of Her Majesty's prisons can develop their self-esteem, then anyone can.

Finally, if you were wondering what happened to Paul, he started his university course in English literature but failed to settle into university life. He attended a forklift truck instructor's course where he obtained his training licences, returned to Holland, married and worked as a foreman in a local family business. A friend of Paul's in prison showed me a postcard he had received from him. In it he expressed the pleasure he received from simply stopping occasionally when driving or walking and admiring the scenery. In the postcard he wrote 'I spent the majority of my life waiting for the big deal that would set me up for life, now I realize I am the big deal and it is for me to set up my own life. Do your rip [finish your sentence] – Paul.'

Chapter 1

Prison Life

The first time I entered a prison was on a guided tour around a young offenders' institute. To my surprise the prisoners looked like how I had imagined them to look. Some had their front teeth missing from fighting, many had badly-drawn tattoos on their arms and often their skin was pasty, which I assumed was from a lack of sun. This is a trait that I still pick up on today when I am interviewing someone outside the prison environment who is vague about their recent history.

The common denominator was the aggressive look they all appeared to wear. Some wore the look due to the cruel life they had been subjected to at such an early age, while others wore it as a defence mechanism against potential predators. I assumed the rest felt obliged to do so in a prison environment.

I was naive enough to believe there was a big difference between the design of a young offenders' institute and an adult prison. There is not. Both have the same statement of purpose: to serve the public by keeping in custody those committed by the courts. The main difference I was to discover over the years was that the adult prison was, on the whole, quiet and peaceful to work in, while the juvenile prison was challenging and often exhausting.

The purpose of my visit was to accompany a group of young people whose behaviour was of concern to the community. They had been identified as people who, without support, might run foul of the law. I had been asked to design a programme and deliver it through a community project. I had identified the areas for concern with the young people. This involved working on their personal-development skills and focusing on their behaviour, communication, teamwork, confidence and self-esteem. The police knew all the young people I was working with and a career in crime was appealing for some. For others, it appeared to be the only avenue open to them to survive. I felt the need for an eye-opener and was able to arrange the prison visit.

The young people glamourized prison as a five-star hotel where all the tough people they knew would eventually book in. The music they bought and the films they watched promoted the image of prison as offering great street credibility. There was no shame in being sent to prison. It was a scar to be proud of.

Walking around the prison I was guilty of looking at the prisoners in their classrooms and training workshops, wondering what hideous crimes they may have committed. I passed judgement on them purely by the way they looked and their body language. The prisoners reciprocated by living up to my expectations and stared at me as though I was invading their privacy, which I guess I was.

We were taken into the art class, which was a hive of activity, and the radio was blaring in the background. I have always found practical subjects popular. Art offers an opportunity to express emotions and feelings and it also appears an easier option if you are not the numerate or literary sort. Another trait of a young offenders' institute, I was to learn, was the amazing ability of the prisoners to cram as many expletives as possible into one sentence. A young man approached us with a steam iron in his hand. The class were doing T-shirt prints. I thought he was going to print something on my head. I stood my ground. He asked me what I wanted and who I was. I asked his name. He offered me his surname only. I explained our visit was an educational one, to help us understand how the prison system worked and take away some ideas to improve our own lives. He laughed, as did all the other prisoners. In unison they asked me the same question: what the hell did I think I could possibly learn from a prison?

Since that day I have not stopped learning from the prison environments and the people who frequent them. It was also the first and last time I addressed a prisoner by their surname only. It made me feel uncomfortable and disempowered me from being able to build a rapport with the person I was speaking to. I have always offered my first name when working with people in prison. I believe it has a relaxing effect. Uniformed staff often work on a surname basis only, which is understandable as they are the disciplinarians; they are the 'screws'.

A brief prison history

It is important to understand the function of prisons, and their evolution is the best place to start. Prisons, as they are portrayed in television programmes and the movies, have been with us for the past 200 years and their origins go back to ancient times. However, they were used not as places for punishment but as holding places for people awaiting trial. Punishment resulting from the trial was often physical and in many cases brutal, including mutilation, whipping and branding. Shaming a person was seen as a popular and effective punishment. Placing them in the stocks (as with other punishments) had an element of entertainment.

Using criminals in a more productive manner by ensuring they worked to pay their debt to society was introduced around the sixteenth century. A cynical person like myself might claim this was an excuse for cheap labour, encouraging 'the powers that be' to sentence more people. The eighteenth century saw the exportation of criminals to the United States and Australia.

An attempt to rehabilitate people rather than punish them was not introduced until 1820, and was practised in the United States. Religion was seen as the saviour for the individual who would be placed in solitary confinement with a Bible, in the hope that they would recognize the error of their ways and repent. The fact that most people committing crimes were illiterate seems to have been overlooked.

In the 1840s prisons were built as places of rehabilitation and were run in a military fashion with strict discipline. The common fear was that by not addressing the needs of these individuals, society would fall victim to violence and corruption.

Corporal punishment was abolished in British prisons in 1967. Those responsible for monitoring the progress of prisoners held the general belief that a cognitive approach was needed. Emphasis was placed on understanding why an individual committed a crime. In theory, prisons were designed to develop the individual in all the areas required to produce a positive member of society. Prisons had been transformed from a place of punishment to a place of rehabilitation. The concept of rehabilitation is key to this book as we explore the ways in which people find themselves in their own prison (or serving their own prison sentence).

Exercise 1: Prison life

Group exercise; see Chapter 15.

What would your prison look like?

Ask yourself what image you conjure up in your mind when you hear the word 'prison' and whether you appear in the image. Is your image from a biblical tale: a Christian in a cage-like prison waiting to face the gladiators in the arena and praying to be saved by God? Do you think of a royal prisoner locked up with all the peasants awaiting their last journey to the guillotine and hoping the Scarlet Pimpernel, dressed as an old woman, will arrive to save them? Do you recall a scene from a Second World War movie set in wooden barracks, with gun towers trained on the occupants, and Tom Cruise as everyone's best buddy prepared to go to solitary confinement on their behalf? If you enjoy a laugh, you may be reminded of a scene from the old comedy *Porridge* where Ronnie Barker saves everyone's bacon. There have been some classic black-and-white movies set in prisons, which always seem to end up with a riot in a large dining hall. Alcatraz is synonymous with the word prison, and some of the best-known gangsters in history, where you need to be extra tough to survive. Your idea of a prison may be more modern, derived from a Hollywood blockbuster where they always have someone trapped on death row, waiting for their beautiful lawyer to save them. Let us not forget those prison officers who are there to ensure no one enjoys their stay. Even though I work in prisons, I still think of a prison as a cold, damp dungeon with rats and people with long beards chained to the wall, begging for more bread and water. I guess this image was formed as a child and has remained with me.

My observations have taught me that prisons are designed with many corridors. Some corridors run through the prison connecting the wings, while other corridors are part of the wing and are lined with cells. Depending on the age of the prison some wings can have cells stacked up to four tiers high. Whatever you imagine prison to be, I would assume that the thought of leaving it is uppermost in your mind. We never imagine a prison as an environment where a person would want to remain. We tend to think of it as a place where we are powerless, where others tell us what we can and cannot do. We sacrifice our first name and instead gain a prison number. It is a place where the process of rehabilitating people is used to recondition the way they think about themselves and the world in which they live, in order to lead fuller lives.

Michael: Street Robbery – three years

Michael was referred to me by his computer teacher to discuss a career in IT as she believed he was a man with hidden potential. He was a loner who did not socialize with the other prisoners and his mood swings made prisoners and staff wary of him. He confided in me that his real ambition was to be an actor and so I arranged for him to attend the drama group. He was an instant success with the other prisoners and the teacher insisted he consider acting as a career. This made life difficult for me as it upset the IT teacher. I asked Michael why, if acting had always been his passion, he had not considered a career in it before. He explained how his father had been a singer, travelling around pubs and social clubs. He never really got to know his father before he died of a drugs overdose. His mother struggled to make ends meet. Aged 13, angry with his mother and father for letting him down, he began shoplifting. Aged 15, his mother's boyfriend came to live with them and Michael's behaviour got worse until he finally left home to live on the streets. From that day on, it was him against the world.

For the past six years he had been in and out of prison and he accepted this as part of his life. What he could not accept was his own prison; the one in his mind that guaranteed his behaviour would return him to a custodial sentence.

Together we explored why he had created his own prison. We realized it was a cocoon he lived in, a place where nothing ever changed and with no expectations of himself, he had no disappointments. The world was a harsh place to exist in. He constantly recalled memories of bad times in his life to justify his present state of mind. This allowed him to get angry both with the people he believed had let him down, and with himself. However, deep down he longed to be a famous actor earning the respect of others. He was denying himself the opportunity to find fulfilment in his life and he needed to release himself from his own prison.

I was able to support his interest in IT and acting and with the help of others we were able to address his concerns. What was most important was that Michael wanted to change. On his release we were able to find him employment in IT with a local charity and Michael joined the local amateur dramatic society. The last I heard about Michael was an e-mail from his probation officer telling me that Michael had been offered and had accepted a position with more money with an IT company back in his home town. He had been in contact with his family who were keen to rebuild their relationship. He was continuing with the acting and attending auditions, but to date he had had no luck. He said he had found it far more difficult breaking free from his own prison than Her Majesty's, but to let others know that it could be done and how wonderful it was.

Disempowerment

People become disempowered when they enter a prison. Hence the idea that you leave a prison the same age you entered it if you just conform to the system and do not look to develop your potential while serving your sentence. This development of maturity must be achieved within the confines of an artificial world where values are categorized with different priorities. What most of us take for granted in the outside world is looked upon with greater appreciation.

I have heard stories of people being attacked for the simplest of items: a cigarette, bottle of shampoo or a bar of chocolate. To the outside world this would appear bizarre. However, in a world where a telephone call is a privilege, I understand why such incidents occur.

This is not to tar all prisoners with the same brush. There are many who tackle their addictions, social dilemmas and behaviour, emerging with a greater understanding of themselves and the world in which they live. These are the areas of development that I believe we can learn from. I meet so many people outside prison who appear to be disempowered, as they do not believe they have any control over their own destiny.

Working in the prison environment for many years has helped me to appreciate the material items in life that we all take for granted. On an average day, walking around a prison to interview prisoners who have requested a meeting or have been referred to me, I might lock and unlock between 50 and 100 gates and doors. At the end of the day when I lock the last door before handing in my keys to go home, I appreciate being able to step into a world where I can do anything I wish, within reason. It is often said that we do not appreciate what we have until we no longer have it. I am sure that almost every person who has been to prison would agree with that statement. The only people who may disagree are those who have nothing in the first instance, which is true of a lot of people who find themselves in a custodial sentence.

So is there anything to be learnt from this world of:

- imprisonment
- disempowerment
- anxiety
- loneliness
- stress
- low self-esteem?

I believe there is. Having the ability to survive all the above would be a bonus in anyone's life. Life in a prison is like an unforgiving experiment in how to survive in the most negative of environments. Not to be able to have learnt something from all this work would be to acknowledge defeat within the system. I believe we can learn a lot about rehabilitating our own lives by studying prison systems and the people within them. I neither condone nor condemn prisoners. I do believe they have enhanced my understanding of human nature and the extremes we can push ourselves to, and, in the majority of cases, unknowingly.

Over the years I have come to realize that the functioning of a prison environment and the policing of its residents are comparable with life outside prison walls, except that there is more attention to detail and discipline of the inhabitants, which is crucial to its success. I have witnessed billions of pounds being spent modifying the prison model to devise the best way to identify the needs of individuals and to support them. Some of the best minds have combined to ensure every attempt is made to rehabilitate people back into society. However, this is not always possible. Adjusting people's perception of themselves and the world they live in is key to the success of any prison. A prisoner's behaviour is monitored daily, and detailed notes are kept. If a prisoner acts inappropriately towards others or themselves, they will be challenged. Ultimately their well-being is the responsibility of the prison service.

Who monitors your well-being? You may not have the attention of others who are able to identify changes in your personality and support you, unless you are fortunate enough to be surrounded by a close circle of friends and family. Even then it is easy to hide your feelings if you wish to do so. Prisoners are observed 24 hours a day, 7 days a week. If a prisoner does not want to participate in any of the following, their well-being will be brought to the attention of the people responsible for their time in custody:

- not wanting to leave their cell
- not eating
- refusing exercise
- not socializing
- being difficult towards others
- being withdrawn and depressed.

You are your own keeper and may drift through negative phases for weeks or months on end without realizing how inappropriate your behaviour has been. What would be worse is being aware of your negative behaviour towards yourself and doing nothing about it. We can all be guilty of not treating ourselves with the love and respect we deserve for a variety of reasons, many of which we may consider out of our control.

In this book I will explore why we treat ourselves this way and attempt to offer solutions. The point I would like to stress is that you may not be responsible for the way you feel about yourself but you could be an accessory to the crime of negative beliefs, and you may be fuelling the fire of discontent when you have the ability to extinguish it. Effectively, you could be classed as a self-harmer: a person who knowingly attacks their well-being. In the next chapter we will look at why you may be an accessory to the crime of negative beliefs. I will explain the cycle you may find yourself in and explore strategies for breaking free.

R U listenin'?

- We are all capable of creating our own prison.

- Your prison will be as harsh as you believe it to be.

- We can learn a lot from being in our own prison.

- You will only stay in your prison if you want to.

- You can release yourself from your prison whenever you wish to do so.

Chapter 2
An Accessory to the Crime

I remember a man who had been known for using a gun in bank robberies. He said he loved nothing more than holding a gat (gun) in his hand. When asked why, he said, 'I felt like I was God; I had the power over life and death.' He explained to me how, when in prison, he would often hold a metaphorical gun of despair against his head. By pulling the trigger he released negative feelings, thoughts and memories of his inability to cope in other similar situations and he would build to a violent rage, attack other prisoners and officers, and eventually find himself in the segregation block. Here he would try to self-harm, or in his words 'Take control of the situation and release the despair I was feeling.' He accepted that he was an accessory to the act of self-harm a 'co-de' (co-defendant, a person charged with aiding and abetting a crime).

Can we self-harm our well-being?

Many professionals accept that self-harm is a way of dealing with intolerable emotional pain. When a person self-harms it may be the only time in their life when they are in control of their own destiny. Self-harming can become a way of life. If we are not careful we can condition ourselves to self-harm as a response to particular situations. Stress is a typical trigger for a lot of people. There is a form of pleasure derived from self-harm. This is not to say that no pain is felt, but the physical pain may not be as great as the emotional pain one might be feeling.

In this chapter I will explore the idea that we could be considered accessories to the crime of self-harm. Not the pain-seeking self-harm we imagine when the word self-harm is mentioned, but the self-harm that attacks our well-being. I will require you to analyse yourself to ensure you are not unknowingly an accessory to the self-harming process. I will pose the question: should a person who attacks their self-esteem either physically or mentally by abusing their bodies with overindulgence in food, drink, lack of exercise, temper tantrums, bullying, bouts of anxiety and negative feelings about themselves *and* make no effort to resolve their behaviour, be viewed as an accessory?

It is important that these pages are not seen as a way of trivializing self-harm. On the contrary, self-harm must been seen as a serious and complex condition. There is evidence to suggest that there is a chemical imbalance in the brain that can cause people to react in this way. However, self-harm does not necessarily stand alone and is often associated with many other disorders.

Exercise 2: An accessory to the crime

Group exercise; see Chapter 15.

Identifying a self-harmer

If a prisoner were identified as being vulnerable to self-harm, measures would be taken to support them. An officer would be appointed to monitor their behaviour. As with anyone in need of support, the officer's role would be as a listener. The officer would discuss issues with specialists in other departments, especially those who know the individual and their history. Involving family members is crucial. However, in reality, some individuals have no family members who are prepared to help, or the individual refuses their support and any attempts to break the cycle. The prisoner's interests are identified, and they are offered options to attend education and other social activities. There are people who offer their services voluntarily to befriend prisoners. They visit and write to the prisoners who respond accordingly. If it was considered appropriate, a visitor may be allocated to the individual and they would also be offered the opportunity to phone the Samaritans. Some prisons have a 'buddy' and 'listener's' scheme where the prisoners are trained to support each other, taking the time to listen and discuss each other's concerns. A change of cell could be an option if it was in the interests of the individual, or a reward system could be introduced to help to ease their tension and focus on other thoughts. The key to the situation is the involvement of each individual in drawing up a plan of support. A review system will show that someone cares and will offer ongoing care while documenting the situation for official purposes.

I work with people who, in my opinion, are damaging their future chances of a contented lifestyle by their current behaviour. Their behaviour disassociates them from society. Many justify their actions by the lack of opportunity offered to them in their life. For some there is evidence for their claim, however, what they fail to appreciate is that the coping strategy they employ to counter-balance their inadequacies is destructive and unnecessary.

Leaving school at an early age and not completing their education leaves some people with major social barriers – in the world of employment, in their family life and often psychologically. They are ill-equipped to deal with many of life's conundrums and often seek alternative ways of coping with stressful situations. They carry negative and ill-informed beliefs about themselves and their ability to achieve contentment. This can only be detrimental to their ability to recognize opportunities, as their vision is clouded by a self-harming approach to dealing with difficult situations. This is not the self-harming that involves cutting or burning oneself, but the self-harming that scars their self-esteem.

A person released from prison may one day stop, re-evaluate their life and decide that a lifetime in and out of prison is not for them. Unfortunately, it is not a case of covering up one's arms with a long-sleeved top to hide any physical scaring. The damage is for all to see in a lack of academic achievement, minimal work experience and a poor CV. Ex-prisoners looking to re-establish their lives may be forced to wear their past as they might wear a tattoo for all to see, every time they go for a job interview, discuss career options, start a relationship or seek a loan.

Balhinder: Shoplifting – six months

One day, a young man I was advising made me promise not to tell anyone in the prison why he had received his custodial sentence. I promised. He then informed me that it was for stealing a pair of underpants, although he did add that they were 'designer' underpants. He told anyone who enquired about his sentence that he was in for car theft. I knew that six months for stealing a pair of underpants was a little harsh and asked him further questions about his offence. I realized the theft was one of many, and it was 'the straw that broke the camel's back' for the judge before whom Balhinder had repeatedly appeared. Balhinder struggled to understand why he had stolen the underpants when he had more than enough money in his pocket to pay for them.

I questioned his emotional state on the day of the theft and he explained that he was anxious. He owed money to a drug dealer who had severely beaten him the week before and was threatening to do the same that week if he did not have the money he owed. I asked if the shoplifting helped to pay his debt. The answer was no. Shoplifting saved him a few pounds – he owed thousands. The further we talked the more I realized that his debt and his shoplifting were related: the greater his debt and fear of violence, the more he felt the need to shoplift. In some cases he shoplifted items he did not want, and on more than one occasion he went straight to the charity shop to donate the item. His shoplifting and donating could have been conceived as a guilt trip – it was not.

It was, in fact, a coping strategy for the stress he was under from the drug dealer. In his despair, he found comfort from shoplifting and an opportunity, for a short while, to release his mind from the constant fear of the drug dealer. He felt successful and in control of the situation. He was, in fact, harming his self-esteem as he participated in actions that would inevitably lead him to a life in prison. Subconsciously he may have seen prison as an escape from the drug dealer – a temporary fix.

Talking to Balhinder it was obvious he had spent his life looking for alternative coping strategies and distractions, instead of accepting his inability to deal with particular situations and learning how to work through them. He stopped going to school at an early age when he found the work difficult, and he became violent when challenged about any beliefs he held ranging from football to his own personal behaviour. Like a lot of people, he had started using drugs as a form of escapism from the life of boredom he had created for himself. He had no coping strategies for situations that made him anxious. What I felt I needed to establish was whether Balhinder realized he was an accessory to the crime of self-harming his well-being and his chances of a contented lifestyle. Did he knowingly behave the way he did? I was not convinced he was aware of what he was doing to himself.

People are unknowing accessories

If we had no feelings for ourselves, we would not receive any satisfaction from our emotions, whether they are positive or negative. Some people may believe that being hard on themselves could be the only time in their life when they do express a healthy self-esteem – a time when they are in control.

I am concerned about people who are not aware that they are accessories or choose to ignore it. We can see the physical damage self-harm does to us whenever we stand on the scales and see the pounds pile on, or get out of breath climbing stairs, and this may be enough to trigger a reaction, which encourages us to change our lifestyle. The mental damage self-harm inflicts may not be so obvious since it attacks our self-esteem on a regular basis.

Ultimately you are the best person to support yourself. We all experience difficult times in our lives. The key is not to be an accessory who invites the crime of 'self-esteem bashing' into their life. Identifying the circumstances in which we become an accessory is crucial to our well-being.

If you live in an environment where people with low self-esteem surround you, you may not appreciate the impact they have on you. Some people believe it is best to think negatively about all outcomes because there are no disappointments in their life when things go wrong. This is a flawed coping mechanism.

The same people do not expect to win when they buy a lottery ticket. When they do not win they are not surprised. They do not appreciate the pleasure and excitement of holding the ticket in their hands as the numbers are announced and dreaming of what they would do with all that money. They feel safer not getting excited because they have no coping mechanisms when they do not win. If they were to get excited and not win, they might consider themselves losers, cry or drown their sorrows in a bottle of wine. It is this type of self-harm that I am looking to address.

Are you an accessory to any of the below?

- talking yourself down

- not taking regular exercise

- eating and drinking too much

- getting angry with others

- feeling lethargic

- wallowing in self-pity

- feeling lonely

- not eating healthy food

- worrying

- wasting valuable time.

There are no set ways of identifying a person who is an accessory. The simple fact is if you are not content with your way of life and make no attempt to change it, but instead fuel your despair, then you are an accessory.

You may believe that you would never be an accessory to self-harm if you thought it would hurt the one you loved. If I was always negative and no fun to be with, my partner would not be happy. However, if I did not have a partner then there would be no one to upset. What about you? Are you not allowed to be upset by the way you are treating yourself?

Consider this scenario. If you do not make the effort to exercise and suffer from heartburn, why do you feel the need to tolerate it? Why not change your diet or exercise? Let us imagine that you get heartburn when you eat chocolate but it is the person you love the most who feels the pain and not you. They beg you not to eat any more chocolate and to exercise. If you really love this person you will probably make the effort. It is now important to realize that you are that person.

Steven: Kidnapping – five years

I first met Steven when a teacher, who was frustrated by his self-destructive attitude, referred him to me. Steven would attend his education classes and he displayed a keen interest in his subjects. However, one could almost guarantee he would never finish his course because he could not control his temper. He would end up in fights with other prisoners or an officer and be removed from his course. On the surface it appeared that he had an anger-management problem.

When I spoke with Steven he was polite and talked enthusiastically about being a car salesman for a large motor company. He was insistent that he 'did not want to work for a small outfit with a reputation for ripping people off.' He had a wife and two children to whom he wanted to be a good father – he did not want his children to lead the life he had.

When he was not in prison he had applied for jobs, but his lack of academic qualifications prevented him from being selected for interviews. His enthusiasm and knowledge about motor cars was obvious but he was told on numerous occasions that he needed qualifications in maths and English for certain aspects of the job. I never doubted Steven's ability to pass his exams – the problem was his temper.

Together we identified the times when he would lose his temper. We quickly realized that it was always in the education block in a classroom situation and, to be more specific, when his exams were looming. Outside education he had a very mature and cognitive approach to potentially volatile situations. What he could not do was cope with the pressure passing exams placed upon him. This was because he had never sat an exam in his life. Passing his exams could potentially change his life. He was an unknowing accessory, destroying his chances of recognizing his ambition. I persuaded Steven that he needed to experience the pressures of exams in a milder setting. We needed to introduce him to coping in stressful situations and show him that his violent reactions were expressions of self-harm.

His tutor set tests for him weekly and we had Steven sit in the classroom where he would eventually take his exam. I acted as an invigilator. We simulated the emotions Steven feared but in a safe environment and discussed his feelings after each session. He eventually achieved his qualifications. Accepting that he was an accessory had helped him to learn how to cope.

Steven realized his goal of being a car salesman. One day I visited him on the forecourt where he worked and we discussed old times, as one does, and who was inside and who was going straight. When I asked Steven about the opportunities that were available to him in the company he was working for, he reminded me of something I had once said to him: an opportunity is like buying a new car; you buy your new car and suddenly you start noticing the same make and colour of car everywhere. You are amazed how many are on the road and wonder why you had never noticed them before – probably because you were not looking for them. He was no longer an accessory to negative thoughts. He had already identified opportunities within the company, set himself some goals and was working towards them.

If, while reading this chapter, you have identified yourself as an accessory – well done. You have identified your negative approach to coping and now you can move forward. The following chapters will offer you some insight into your behaviour. I am a firm believer that an understanding of our behaviour empowers us with the knowledge we need in order to address and change any negative beliefs we hold about ourselves, thus allowing us to lead a contented lifestyle.

Our next chapter explores the concept that a prisoner serving a sentence is aware of the crime they have been charged with. The length of sentence has been agreed by the court, allowing them to plan their life around the sentence. You, on the other hand, may not be aware of committing any crime but feel sentenced to a life of minimum contentment, unaware of the length of your sentence and unable to appeal. We will explore where your beliefs came from and look at ways you can address those beliefs which are preventing you from enjoying a healthy well-being.

R U listenin'?

- Monitor your behaviour in relation to your emotions. This could indicate that you may be an accessory.

- An accessory is a person whose coping strategy attacks their well-being.

- No one is perfect. We all have bad habits – the key is to control them.

- Do not engage with people who fuel your negative feelings.

- Ensure that you are eating a healthy diet and exercising regularly.

Chapter 3

Believing your Way Out from Within

 I enjoy facilitating group discussions and 'belief' is always a good subject to debate. I asked one group for their thoughts on the subject and they automatically assumed I was referring to religious belief, which is the case with most people when you mention the word 'belief'. They responded by saying they were disappointed in God. Why had He allowed them to lead lives that no person in their right mind would voluntarily choose, while allowing others to live comfortable lives with happy families and money?

One prisoner within the group, who obviously had a strong belief in God, was shouting and banging the table like an Evangelical preacher. He said that it was not for God to save prisoners – it was the responsibility of prisoners to believe in Jesus and follow His teachings. He went on to quote the following passage, claiming it was never too late to believe:

> Then one of the criminals who was hanged blasphemed him, saying, 'If you are the Christ save yourself and us.'
>
> But the other answering rebuked him, saying, 'Do you not even fear God, seeing you are under the same condemnation?
>
> And we indeed justly, for we receive the due rewards of our deeds: but this man has done nothing wrong.'
>
> Then he said to Jesus, 'Lord, remember me when you come into your kingdom.'
>
> And Jesus said to him, 'Assuredly, I say to you, today you will be with me in paradise.' (Luke 23: 39–43 New King James version)

I asked how he knew if the criminal on the cross really believed or was just covering all bases. He thought about it for a while and replied, 'Because I am a criminal on my own cross and I too have learnt to believe.' There are times in prison when one can be profoundly moved, and this, for me, was one of those moments.

Many of the men I work with in prison are able to inform me of their religious belief. The majority have lapsed but some are keen to practise their religion whilst serving their sentence. Unfortunately for their victims, however, they were not so keen to 'practise' when they committed the crime.

People often discover religion in prison; it's a good place to find it. When you have time to think about your life, then religion frequently has the answers to many questions. Following a religious way of life is easier when you have few distractions and temptations, but now I am digressing into a chapter about religion when I want to use this chapter to explore the concept of belief, not religion. Belief can come in many forms and can have many meanings. It will help us throughout our life, offering guidance when the present looks bleak and the future disastrous. I am interested in the belief that we have within ourselves to recognize and realize greater contentment.

If you believe in this book's message about your ability to develop your own self-esteem for a healthier well-being, then it will be a useful tool for you to reference when life is not going to plan. If you do not believe in this book and do not take the advice it offers, what will be your alternative? Remember, having negative beliefs about ourselves is a belief in itself.

How does the brain believe?

The brain uses the senses of smell, taste, touch, sight and hearing for survival. These senses act as the brain's informers when it is contemplating a decision, and all decisions have 'survival' as their common denominator. When driving a car we are using our senses to identify specific actions required for safety. Senses have their limitations in terms of their range and so the brain requires another system to advise us on what we cannot smell, taste, touch, see or hear, and that system is 'belief'.

A fireman entering a building on fire in the middle of the night looking for a lost child is acutely aware of the dangers he faces. They are based on his beliefs about what could happen to him if he is careless and rushes into rooms where floors and ceilings could collapse. His best tool for survival in this situation is his belief. If he believes in all the training he has received and his own ability to act on his beliefs, he has a good chance of surviving and rescuing the child. His belief is extending the range of his senses. He has become more sensitive to danger, and his brain is working overtime to ensure his survival. The brain is drawing on beliefs it has mapped for the parts of the world it is not able to contact with its senses.

We have many beliefs that are not based on our sensory data, for example, I do not understand how my computer works. My belief in the ability of a micro-chip to make it respond to my commands assists me. Without belief I would be limited to the here and now, living only in the space I occupy at any moment in time, and unable to perceive anything beyond my sensory data. With belief I am able to accept meanings, reasons and causes. Beliefs are independent of my sensory data and they are there for a reason – primarily for my survival. It is important that they have the ability to survive even when contradictory evidence is presented by others or by our senses.

Exercise 3: Believing your way out from within

Group and individual exercise; see Chapter 15.

Zak: Threatening Behaviour – three years

I met Zak after a session I had completed about belief. He explained how he had lost his ability to believe in anyone, including himself, for many years. I was curious and asked him why. Zak told me he had a stable background up to the age of 13 when suddenly his world fell apart. His father was killed falling from a crane while he was at work. At the inquest it emerged that he had been having an affair with a female member of staff and that both were planning to leave their families and start a new life together. They had been drinking heavily at lunchtime, and returned to work drunk. This substantially affected his father's judgement and subsequently affected the insurance payout. Zak, his mother and his three brothers found themselves struggling to pay the bills, and eventu-ally they had to sell their home and move to a council flat.

Zak lost his belief in the authorities who, in his opinion, had cheated his family of his financial security. He also lost belief in the person who was his role model: his father. He was about to embark on a life that would attack every-thing his parents had raised him to respect. Zak turned to petty crime, pro-gressing eventually to joining a notorious street gang.

Ironically, he believed that joining the gang and participating in their ritualis-tic beliefs saved his life. It gave him a sense of belonging as he found friendship and common interests and it filled many of the gaps left by his father's death. Maturity, complemented with many prison sentences, had made him realize that the gang offered him the opportunity to fulfil the needs we all have, namely the need to believe in himself and his ability to be part of a society. His prison sentences had given him the time to re-evaluate his life, and he realized it was not wrong to feel the needs he felt. It was *how* he fulfilled his needs that had been wrong.

Producing volumes of data to disapprove a belief is fruitless unless we can identify the impact the belief has on our survival and what we are able to replace it with. For example: if a person leads a life of contentment believing in the afterlife whenever they are feeling negative, and I produce evidence to disprove their belief, why would they want to believe my evidence? Doing so might take away the comfort they receive from believing in the afterlife, leaving them with nothing when they are feeling negative. You may now see the danger of taking away a person's belief, if you have nothing to replace it. People are not wrong to have beliefs that others may view as stupid. In Zak's case it was gaining an awareness of his needs and learning how to replace inaccurate beliefs with positive, fulfilling beliefs. Beliefs can be seen as the brain's last stance – it will defend them to the end.

Beliefs can contradict each other

We use our senses and beliefs to complement each other. However, they do not have to agree with each other, hence the reason we can believe in the supernatural or science fiction, for which there may be no credible evidence. Evidence does not have preference over belief, as long as the brain's belief forms part of its survival, it will side with belief. You could produce a library full of evidence to disprove the existence of guardian angels, but ask the soldier who is going into battle, who may believe his guardian angel will ensure his survival, to accept the evidence. My guess is he will reject it. His belief in his guardian angel increases his chances of survival whereas accepting the evidence decreases his chances of survival. Belief will have preference over evidence where survival is concerned.

Take the artists who spend their lives believing that they will be famous one day. Numerous agents inform them that they do not have the necessary talent but they continue chasing their dream regardless. Their belief is getting them out of bed everyday fighting for survival and as the brain is content with survival, it sees no reason to challenge the evidence. Remember, if you take a person's belief away and you have nothing to replace it with, you may do more damage than good. How many times have you heard of a person turning to drink and drugs, often because they have lost the reason they had for living – they had lost their belief.

To change an individual's belief and what it stands for, would not only alter an individual's perception, it would destroy their trust in themselves to rely on their own beliefs. Ultimately, it could have a detrimental effect on their survival.

Beliefs do not occur in isolation – they are related to one another. Locked together, they present us with a view of the world as we see and experience it. They offer us the consistency, control and cohesion we require to survive. To accept that a particular belief you have held for a long time is incorrect, no matter how small the belief, would mean undermining all beliefs. Hence the reason why many people defend their beliefs even in the face of overwhelming evidence, including death.

A lot of the people I advise often identify a person or people who they believe have let them down at some point in their lives and they now struggle to believe in anyone. This makes my job all the more difficult because their belief system has been proven not to be reliable. You may have heard a friend telling you never to believe anything a second-hand car salesman tells you. They base this information on their experience of buying a car that fell apart from a second-hand car salesman. This is an example of someone whose belief system, in their opinion, has let them down. Their confidence in their belief system has been put into question, especially where money is concerned.

Sean: Murder – 25 years

Sean had a self-fulfilling prophecy. He believed that one day he would find himself serving a long prison sentence and this belief gave him a licence to behave as he wished. He had accepted his fate and was not surprised when he eventually received a life sentence for killing another man over a drug deal. When he was sentenced he said it was almost a sense of relief, as he knew his lifestyle would lead him to prison and he felt powerless to prevent it.

When a person is locked into a belief that has no reasoning to it, it is difficult to reason them out of it. Attempts had been made by probation and family members to change Sean's belief but all were met with aggression. He had no credible reason for his belief. Only after the event, and many years into his sentence, was he able to accept that his belief about serving a long prison sentence was based on the belief of others. His mother, on regular occasions, had reminded him that he was just like his father who was also serving a long prison sentence. A belief he had accepted and then used to hide behind resulted in him leading a life of anarchy. At one point he tailored his star sign to fit in with his self-fulfilling prophecy and had 'born to serve a sentence' tattooed on his arm. He did what a lot of people do, he managed to convince himself about his inevitable fate and lead his life accordingly.

Are you like Sean? Do you have a self-fulfilling prophecy that dictates you will never find contentment in your life? Do you treat yourself inappropriately, justifying your actions by claiming that you will never receive a promotion, earn more money or meet the perfect partner? Have you given up on yourself because of inaccurate beliefs you cling onto and in some cases hide behind?

Beliefs come in many shapes

Belief is an important part of our make-up; what we believe and why, are debatable. If your beliefs help you through the day without attacking your self-esteem then your beliefs will only serve to enhance your well-being. The following are some superstitious beliefs, or are they?

- You must get out of bed the same side you got in or you will have bad luck.

- The sound of bells drives away demons because they are afraid of bells.

- If a clock which has not been working suddenly chimes, there will be a death in the family.

- Pulling out a grey hair will cause ten more to grow in its place.

- It is bad luck to walk under a ladder.

- Breaking a mirror results in seven years' bad luck.

- A rabbit's foot will bring luck and protect the owner from evil spirits if carried in the pocket.

- All wishes on shooting stars come true.

- Knock on wood three times after mentioning good fortune so evil spirits won't ruin it.

We all have the ability to believe. What I find intriguing is the ability to have a belief that has no evidence to substantiate it. In fact there may be evidence to disprove it and people still believe it even when the belief is destructive to their own well-being or the lives of others. People outside the prison environment can rarely comprehend why some people commit crimes. In many cases I have identified 'belief' as the reason. They believe they have no choice in their life, functioning on survival instincts only. Up to a point I appreciate their dilemma.

When explaining to groups outside the prison environment why people who commit crimes literally believe crime is their vocation in life, I often use what I call my 'door' theory. The idea behind the door theory is to imagine that when you are born you are given the opportunity to choose the life you wish to lead. You are confronted by a series of doors marked A–Z with different lifestyles planned out on each door. You simply enter through the door you wish your life to follow. The point I am trying to emphasize is that as children we are not in a position to choose which of life's doors we enter. Our guardians will determine this and the environment we are raised in. However, the door we enter will influence our belief system.

DOOR A	DOOR B
Family Education Career Security Health Self-esteem Respect	No family Poor education No career prospects No security Low self-esteem

The key to this dilemma is appreciating what you believe was written on your door and who the hell did the writing. You may consider door B to be the negative door and door A to be the positive door. I am suggesting that people who entered through door B are none the wiser about their own lifestyle regardless of how destructive it might be, because they have never experienced the lifestyle of the people who entered the remaining doors. I can try to imagine what it must feel like to serve a prison sentence or live in a mansion but I will never truly know until I have experienced it.

If you accept that the majority of your beliefs are learnt from your guardians and the environment you are raised in, then you are in a position to recognize where many of your current beliefs come from.

In the next chapter we will concentrate on these issues. We will consider the possibility that the beliefs others have instilled in us, and some misconceptions we have about ourselves, may have acted as judge and jury. We have been sentenced to a set of beliefs about ourselves and our ability to achieve. These beliefs are potentially inaccurate and in some cases are downright lies.

I began this chapter by mentioning a group discussion I had been involved in about religion and so I thought I would end on a religious note. In the Catholic religion there is a prayer to the Virgin Mary, and one line in the prayer states 'Pray for us in this our final hour'. If you think about it we are always in the final hour of our life. The expression 'take life a day at a time' is quite poignant. Taking life an hour at a time is all we can manage sometimes and that is not such a bad idea. As we are always in our last hour why not make the most of it? We should remember that an hour can extend to a day, then a week, a month, a year and eventually a lifetime.

R U listenin'?

- Without belief we are trapped in the here and now.

- You do not have to be religious to believe.

- Belief is a wonderful friend and a dangerous enemy.

- Belief comes in many shapes and sizes.

- If you do not believe in yourself, why would anyone else believe in you?

- Belief has the power to make or break our self-esteem.

Chapter 4

Knowing your Sentence

 Having worked with prisoners sentenced for every conceivable crime, I am often asked the following questions, by friends and colleagues:

1. Have you worked with a murderer?
2. Were you scared?
3. How is a sentence determined?
4. How do they decide where a sentence is served?

My answers are:

1. Yes. However, I feel the need to point out that I have worked with a lot of people who I believe have the potential to murder and one day might do so. The fact that they have not already murdered is more to do with luck than a conscious act.

2. No, I would definitely not be able to do the job if I was scared. I am no hero and I am even less of a fool! Should I find myself in an uncomfortable situation, I would get myself out of it. I could end an interview politely, stand up and walk away, press the panic button on the wall or blow my whistle. Ultimately, keeping myself fit and healthy and priding myself on my ability to out-run a lot of people half my age contributes to ensuring my safety.

3. Various factors determine the length of time an individual must spend in prison, including the severity of a prisoner's crime and their age. However, the main criteria for determining the length of a sentence are:

• The length of tariff (the tariff is the part of a sentence that must be served).

- The individual's ability to deal with their own behavioural problems.

- Whether they are considered a risk to the public.

- The potential level of risk they present to the public.

When released, a prisoner serving a life sentence will be 'on licence' for the rest of their lives. However, someone who is in for burglary and has been sentenced for a year rather than life for example, could have a tariff of eight months followed by a further four months 'on tag'. 'Tag' is an electronic chip and comes in the form of a large watch, which is strapped to the leg. This is designed to monitor individuals' movements, which are then reported directly to a central control station. Most of these people will be on curfew and failure to comply may result in them returning to prison for breaking the conditions of their licence. Regardless of the crime the have committed the same licence conditions apply to everyone and, in the majority of cases, if you break your licence conditions, you will be returned to prison.

4. Age, sex and their level of risk to the public will determine where prisoners will serve their sentence. Adult male prisons are graded by security.

- Category prison A (maximum security, for high-risk prisoners)

- Category prison B (secure prison)

- Category prison C (training prison)

- Category D (open prison, no perimeter walls).

 How a sentence is determined is the question which interests me most. In the last chapter we explored the idea that beliefs influence the way we lead our lives and I believe a lot of people live out their own negative sentences because of inaccurate beliefs they have collected about themselves. They feel unable to recognize their true potential. What concerns me most is when a person, who considers themselves sentenced by negative beliefs, has no idea of how long they have been sentenced for and how much longer their sentence has to run.

A prisoner in one of Her Majesty's prisons has the luxury of knowing why they were sentenced and also the length of sentence including any time off due to good behaviour, and this, in itself, can be comforting to them. This provides them with a time period in which they can work on their concerns and plan for their future.

When a prisoner is nearing the end of their sentence, a programme is put together to prepare them for their release. Adjusting to a life outside prison is traumatic and for some, too much to cope with, especially after spending so many years being told what to do and when to do it. For many individuals, decision-making can become an almost impossible task. Being locked in a cell for months, and in some cases years, denies a person the opportunity to achieve. Achieving any given task whether it is building a garden fence, running a marathon or washing the car can all help to maintain a healthy self-esteem.

Exercise 4: Knowing your sentence

Group and individual exercise; see Chapter 15.

Are you serving a sentence?

Working in prisons I constantly hear the same statement from inmates: 'I am not coming back.' However, I do see the same faces returning, and in most cases, sadly, I am not at all surprised to see them. So why don't people learn from their mistakes? Maybe they do not really see what they are doing as mistakes? Maybe they are accepting what they do as the norm, a way of life, or perhaps they even believe they have no control over their own destiny and it is out of their hands?

Consider the following:

A prisoner in a category A high-security prison with minimal privileges may accept that the life they lead has its risks, one of which is to receive a custodial sentence if they are caught. They recognize themselves in the mirror as a burglar, bank robber or thug and are comfortable with what they see. They view their victims as 'opportunities' for them to take advantage of.

Now consider the prisoner in a category D open prison in a very relaxed atmosphere with lots of privileges. They look in the mirror and are ashamed of what they see. They cannot believe they are a burglar, bank robber or con man, even if they have been sentenced for one of these crimes and have admitted their guilt, because this is not what they wanted for themselves from life. They show genuine remorse towards their victims and wonder how they have ended up in this predicament.

The point I am trying to stress in this scenario is a person in a comfortable environment physically is not necessarily in a comfortable state of mind mentally. It depends on what they want from their life. If they accept they are a criminal and nothing can change them then they will live their life accordingly. If they believe they could be a valuable member of society but find themselves serving a prison sentence, they will be hard on themselves. This is not a bad thing as long as they are proactive in changing the predicament they find themselves in. They are physically serving one sentence and so there is no need to serve another mentally. Can you relate to their predicament?

I regularly meet people who have sentenced themselves to a prison within their own minds; they feel trapped and are unable to recognize their true potential. Some knowingly commit the offence as it offers them comfort, and they use their inaccurate beliefs as boundaries which they are not prepared to push. Unfortunately, in the majority of cases they are not aware of their behaviour.

They occasionally escape from their inaccurate beliefs about their inability to lead a full and constructive life, only to be recaptured by a passing emotion which could be triggered by a variety of events, such as a comment or action by another person, a television programme, a smell or a memory. Any of these can return the individual to the same negative beliefs that formed their sentence. As for the category of prison people place themselves in, this can range from category A (no foreseeable escape) to category D (a prison with no walls).

Andy: Grievous Bodily Harm (GBH) – three years

Andy considered himself to be the loneliest man on the planet with no real friends or anyone to confide in. He was a man with a violent nature, which he believed was a necessary evil if he was to maintain his dignity. Because he believed violence was a necessity in his life, he found it difficult to make friends and keep them. He failed to realize that his aggressive attitude provoked others.

There was a period in Andy's life when he was not lonely. He had a relationship with a lady called Susan and after one year together Susan gave birth to their daughter. Unfortunately things did not work out and the relationship ended. Andy was devastated because not only was he back to being the loneliest person on the planet but he was now, also, the worst partner and father. He began drinking heavily and one night became involved in an argument with another man in a bar, which resulted in him hitting the man with a bottle and fracturing his skull.

Talking to Andy in prison about his statement that he was the 'loneliest man on the planet', I discovered that as a child he was often ridiculed at school. Teachers gave him low marks in exams, detention and extra homework. At an early age he realized that what he lacked mentally he made up for physically. His quick temper and large physique made him a threat to teachers and pupils and his school attendance proceeded to become erratic as his anger towards authority grew. He blamed all his problems on the people at school who, in his opinion, had rejected him, most notably the teachers who made his life difficult by criticizing his work and implying he needed more one-to-one tuition than other learners. In his opinion they had failed him – it was their fault he felt the need to be aggressive and had no friends.

Andy was guilty of the crime he had been sentenced for and he was also guilty of hiding behind a false set of beliefs. As is the case with a lot of people, he did not ask for his particular set of beliefs, in part they were imposed upon him via the negative comments made by others and his failure to recognize the support people were trying to offer him.

Together we identified that Andy's aggression made up for what he considered were the inadequacies in his life. By removing these inadequacies I believed Andy's anger would be less likely to be triggered. Andy was tested and confirmed as being dyslexic and this offered him the opportunity to realize that there had been a reason for his low academic achievements. With the right support he began to achieve academically. He addressed his dyslexia while in prison and started a bricklaying course. He was able to draw up a list of goals, which was something he had not been in a position to do before.

Andy was shipped out (moved to another prison) and, before leaving, was able to negotiate with the governor of the prison that he would continue to receive the support he needed with his dyslexia. Unfortunately, the prison he was moved to did not deliver courses in bricklaying but he was given a place on a painting and decorating course that allowed him to learn a practical skill and continue to work on his dyslexia.

I met with Andy a few months after his release. He did not have a full-time job but he was getting occasional construction work from agencies. I asked him if he was still the loneliest man on the planet. He told me he was not. He was working as a volunteer in an adult literacy evening class, had regular contact with his daughter and was in a new relationship. He was an avid reader and told me, 'You can never be lonely when you can read a good book.' Andy appeared to be a more contented person because he had been able to identify where his negative beliefs stemmed from and had addressed them.

Where do sentences come from?

Do you ever start the day with a well-rehearsed speech – the one that guarantees you start your day in a negative mood? You're constantly reminding yourself how slow you are at performing tasks, or how weak-willed you are when confronted by a large slice of strawberry gateau. You may question: is this my life, or is it a dream I will wake from? It may well be a dream if you realize that the majority of the negative beliefs you hold are created by yourself in your mind and are based on comments directed at you by people at work or within a social environment and which are actually fictitious. By accepting these beliefs, nurturing them over many years and being unable to deal with personal hang-ups which you may be responsible for, will almost certainly guarantee you sentencing yourself to periods of low self-esteem.

If we accept that we do sentence ourselves and limit our potential for contentment through thoughts and beliefs about ourselves, then we need to decide if we chose our sentence or did someone pass judgement on us? Let us assume that we are responsible for our own sentence. Why would we allow ourselves to be sentenced to a life of negative beliefs about our own abilities, waking up in the morning only to criticize ourselves? Simple – we believe we deserve it.

Take the person who has just been sacked from their job because they were constantly late. Their response could be as follows: I have always had a punctuality problem. So, the questions they need to ask themselves are:

- Why have I always had a punctuality problem?
- What gives me the right to have a punctuality problem?
- Why don't I change if it is costing me my job?
- Am I a prisoner who has accepted their fate?
- Do I want to change?
- If I do, how will this affect my belief system about myself?
- Will it undermine every belief I have ever held about myself?

The last question is the killer blow: what will happen to me if I prove I have the ability to change a belief I have held all my life?

Simon: Drug Dealer – four years

I regularly work with people who have hang-ups about their self-image. Simon had average grades from school, but considered himself 'simple' because his three brothers all achieved higher grades and went to university. In their infinite wisdom they christened him 'Simple Simon'. He had not recognized his true potential, but instead had lived up to the Simple Simon name his brothers had given him. He presented himself as a low-achiever and a simple person who would do anything for a laugh. Unfortunately this included taking and eventually selling drugs to pay for his habit.

Simon's belief that he was a simple person had prevented him from taking his responsibilities seriously and he had drifted away from his family refusing every course or job offered to him. He had become scared of achieving anything, as this would contradict every belief he had held about himself throughout his life. At first, changing Simon's beliefs about himself was a difficult task for me and, ultimately, a painful one for him. I encouraged him to take qualifications in a variety of subjects while he was in prison and he also managed to get himself a job in the prison storeroom where he was responsible for issuing the prisoners' kit. He continued achieving and worked really hard to retain his job (jobs are always sought after in prisons) and to his horror he realized he actually enjoyed studying and working. He began to lose his identity as the 'non-achiever', 'the clown' and he then began to feel confused. This confusion turned to anger as he reflected upon his life and the time he had wasted.

I met with Simon's brothers and explained where I believed his set of beliefs about himself had come from. They all felt guilty and agreed with my observations – they had not realized what Simon was putting himself through. When he was eligible for a community visit (an opportunity for a prisoner to leave the prison for the day to visit a place close by with a relative), Simon's oldest brother spent the day with him. This visit was encouraging and when Simon left prison he did so with a new confidence. His family supported him and ensured he was involved in all family occasions. Unlike a lot of people I see leaving prison, Simon was very fortunate in being able to return to a loving family who supported him.

Unfortunately he eventually returned to prison – his drug addiction was a greater demon than his beliefs. I was convinced his beliefs (or misbeliefs) about his ability to lead a constructive life had led him into the meaningless life he endured. Changing his beliefs had been of benefit, but his drug addiction was a battle I was not trained to help him with.

 To address a belief, we first need to identify where our beliefs come from. There is a comfort factor in knowing who you are and what you can and cannot achieve. Whether you are the bloke who loves football, drinks lots of beer and likes a flutter on the horses, or the businessman who is ambitious and dreams of owning his own company, it is a way of building our boundaries and helps us to respond to given situations. The intelligent young boy who is expected to do well in his exams will, in the majority of cases, work hard to live up to his beliefs and the beliefs of his guardians and teachers. The lazy young boy, however, who believes himself to be too stupid to pass any exam and too lazy to study will achieve low grades as predicted. Each boy will respond according to his own beliefs and those of other people.

Many beliefs we have about ourselves are based on statements we have adopted from our childhood and continue to reinforce when we consider it appropriate. The statement 'I will never change, I have always been this way' is often used – it is a common excuse for refusing to make an effort to change a negative attribute. We soak information up daily, both consciously and subconsciously absorbing other people's comments about ourselves and the world around us. As children we are more inclined to believe what we are told by our peers, parents, relatives and schoolteachers. Comments about the way we look and behave are internalized by us and they become part of our self-image, affecting the way in which we perceive ourselves.

When a person informs me they are not happy I automatically ask them what would make them happy. If they tell me they do not know, I ask them how they know they are unhappy. When a person tells you they are hungry you assume they should know, if you ask them, what they would like to eat. They may need to consider your question and the options available on the menu but ultimately they will take a decision and feed their hunger.

We all have answers to the questions about our behaviour and beliefs. Often they are beliefs we have collected throughout our lives and it would be wrong to suggest you simply discard your beliefs. Some beliefs are about our ability to achieve, while others are negative, like our ability to underachieve. Many successful people will accredit their success to having belief in their own ability as due to positive nurturing received throughout their childhood. These are often our most treasured beliefs and will play a major role in the development of future beliefs. This is not to say we cannot collect beliefs at any stage in our lives: we can.

Try identifying where your beliefs come from. You may have been messy, naughty and insecure as a child with lots of red crosses in your schoolbooks to prove it. This does not mean you have to be a messy, naughty and insecure adult. You may have developed your personality to respond to your set of beliefs.

A prisoner recalls the neighbours in his street who predicted he would end up in prison one day. Were they correct? Or has he just accepted their beliefs and lived his life accordingly. Standing in front of a judge in the dock and being told he is a criminal, he smiles and announces, 'Everyone knows I am a criminal. I burgle houses and sell drugs.' This is an example of a person who uses their beliefs as an excuse to reject their responsibility to themselves and society. We can all be guilty of living up to other people's beliefs about ourselves. Depending on how much we feel the need to seek their approval they can influence our career decisions, the type of partner we choose and our friends.

I regularly surprise people when I inform them that I have the same negative beliefs they have. They wonder why I do not practise what I preach – I do. If the belief affects my well-being, I tackle it immediately. If the belief is about my inability to drive from A to B without getting lost, it is a belief I accept for now. One day I will buy a quality road map or work my routes out on the Internet, or just simply buy a guidance system for my car; I know I have the ability to dispose of the belief. For the moment I hide behind it, using it as an excuse when I am late for meetings!

A point I will stress in this book is that we are not the complex machines some people would have us believe. Physically we are truly an amazing achievement but mentally we exaggerate our individuality. If you had a conversation about your negative beliefs with another person who lived in an igloo at the North Pole they would probably have similar ones to yours.

In the next chapter we will look at the needs we have in our lives that are natural. They are genetically-triggered needs and we are driven by our genes to fulfil them. You may have spent your life to date dreaming of sharing your life with a beautiful partner, children, and a pet in a comfortable home. The next chapter will explain why you have these dreams and why you're not the only person to have them.

R U listenin'?

- Your life is not a prison sentence.

- When you understand where a belief comes from you are able to address it.

- Do not use your beliefs as excuses for not leading the life you want.

- If you have a belief that is affecting your well-being address it now.

- Remember, not all beliefs are negative.

- Create the beliefs you want for yourself – they're called goals.

Chapter 5
Natural Instincts

 'Association' is a period of time when prisoners are permitted to socialize with each other on the wing and it is normally allowed in the evening or at weekends. During this time, some will play various games, such as pool or table tennis while others will concentrate on their hobbies or watch television. Television is a good source of both entertainment and education within a prison and for some it is the only contact with the outside world. This can, however, limit a prisoner's understanding of topical subjects depending on what programmes they watch.

Discussions about previous nights' programmes are common as in any work place or school playground. Facts to back up debates are often limited to the programme and this, combined with some creative thinking on behalf of the debaters (who often suffer from limited knowledge on the subject), can make for some highly-charged discussions. Some prisoners believe a one-hour programme will offer all the information necessary to be an expert on a given subject. Others are more inquisitive and will order library books in order to explore the subject further. Some will even contemplate studying given subjects based on an interest that has been sparked by a programme.

Delivering training in personal development often means addressing very sensitive issues, which need to be treated with the utmost care for the participants and the facilitator. In many of the environments I have worked in, television programmes have been responsible for heated debates, which can be potential hot spots for explosive confrontations. I credit myself with a sixth sense, which I have developed over the years, that helps me identify and defuse any potential outbreaks of violence.

However, there was an occasion when the training room was like a scene from a spaghetti western film. The only excuse I can offer was the fact that I was so engrossed in a debate that I did not see the trouble coming. Fists and chairs flew around the room, as I did my Spiderman impersonation of crawling around the training room walls to reach the panic button. All this was over a disagreement about a pair of genes. The genes in question were the criminal gene and the homosexual gene.

The discussion started during a training session I was delivering on the subject of nature versus nurture. Are we born with criminal traits or do they develop in the environments in which we are raised? Do we have any say in our lives or will our genes dictate our life plan? The prisoners began to discuss a programme they had watched on TV about genes and the possible discovery of the criminal gene. If it was ever proven to exist, the implications in a court of law could potentially result in people walking free, or having their sentences reduced.

A prisoner in the class had decided that this was the reason for him being a criminal. He had watched the programme and decided he had inherited the criminal gene, which had multiplied within his system causing him to lead a life of crime. He delivered a profound speech on the life his genes had forced him to lead. I could see he had sparked the imagination of other prisoners as they began to compare their criminal history with his and confirm their belief that they too had been victims of their own genes.

Theories began to run riot when another prisoner mentioned a programme he had watched that discussed the finding of the homosexual gene, which, under the microscope, looked very similar to the criminal gene. This initially caused an abrupt halt to the discussion as everyone pondered its implications. The prisoner (whose intention was to cause trouble) then suggested that the other prisoners did not have the criminal gene, but probably had the homosexual gene. Before I could derail his insinuation by informing everyone that we have thousands of genes in our bodies and no one has identified a criminal or homosexual gene, the 'aggressive gene' had taken control and there was chaos.

 So, was there any truth in the genes discussion (riot). There is scientific evidence that genes dictate our biological features. But are they responsible for our behaviour or is behaviour learnt from the environment we are raised in? It is a debate that goes back centuries.

Some scientists believe that behaviour may be dictated by our genetic makeup while others believe that genes may be turned on and off by the environment they find themselves in. On a personal note and as a layperson whose knowledge of genetics could be etched on the back of a postage stamp, I am in favour of the latter idea, that genes are regulated by the lifestyle we lead. It's my hope that a person leading a healthy well-balanced life style with a positive outlook on life may trigger different responses at the genetic level to the person who abuses their body and harbours negative beliefs.

A common argument used to debunk the idea that genes dictate our behaviour is the example of the identical twins raised in different environments who share similar behaviour traits. There could be evidence to show they may have similar interest in playing basketball, eating pizza and dating girls. This could possibly be because they are both 6ft 6", a lot of young people enjoy eating pizza and they are both heterosexual males. If both rejected the boundaries of a society, committed similar crimes, rejected the responsibilities of maturity and lived in similar houses one might have a case for the genetic argument.

Exercise 5: Natural instincts

Group and individual exercise; see Chapter 15.

Vernon: Street Robbery – 18 months

Vernon attended a session I delivered in a young offenders' institute on career opportunities. The session materialized the way it always did, with me in front of the class with the white board on the wall behind me, full of positive options the young men could try to help them gain employment. The young men (eight in total) were sitting in front of me being negative and coming up with every reason they could think of why they would never find employment. Despite the fact that they built barriers to every suggestion I made, I felt I had the upper hand, mainly because the average age of these young men was 19, and I, on the other hand, had years of experience running such sessions. Consequently, I had heard all the excuses for not finding employment before and so I was able to knock down all their barriers. Their suggestions for their 'ideal' job were the usual: porn star, bank manager and my job, because it looked a 'cushy number'. On completion of the session I made my usual offer of inviting them (if they wished) to apply for some one-to-one careers advice and guidance. In order to get this, they would need to complete a governor's app (governor's application form). If a prisoner has a request, they complete a governor's application form which, in turn, is sent to the appropriate body.

It was difficult not to remember Vernon as he sat through the whole session in silence. He was a big, black guy whose eyes pierced through your head when he looked at you. I always felt Vernon was looking at my brain when we spoke, seeking to detect any lies I might concoct. He had completed a governor's application form requesting advice on a college course and so I went to his wing to meet and have a chat with him. He sat opposite me in an empty classroom with his fixed stare and informed me that he wanted to be a rap artist. He had been writing lyrics about his life on the road and believed that they would make him a big rap artist. Talking to Vernon, I quickly established that he could not play a musical instrument and, to date, had shown no interest in any form of music at all. I sat there and thought – oh no, not another young man with no musical talent whatsoever who wants to be a gangster rap star, and then I got worried in case he could actually look at my brain and work out what I was thinking!

As with any request, I have to explore the options; it is not my job to judge people or in any way dismiss any ideas they might have. Vernon talked about the lyrics he had been writing in his cell, which were based on his life to date, and I asked to see the work as a way of judging his sincerity and ability. I took his work away to read through and to do some investigating into the music industry.

Reading through Vernon's lyrics I began to build a picture of a young man who, in his short life, had tasted the depths of despair. He had come to England from the United States at an early age with a person he believed to be his uncle but he was never too sure. This person later died – again he was not too sure why – but he believed it may have been from Aids. He then went to live with a person who claimed to be his mother. He was very happy at this point and pleased to have a mother. Over the next ten years (with the person he called his mother) he moved from one flat to another and on some occasions from one squat to another. There were a string of uncles and people passing through their home; some were nice to him but others shouted and hit him. At the age of 14 he decided it was best to leave home for his own safety, because the person he called mother had a new boyfriend who was violent and who consumed large quantities of drugs.

Over the next two years he survived on the streets sleeping anywhere from bus shelters, doorways and parks, to the backs of cars he had stolen. He discovered all the shelters where he could get handouts of food. He lied about his age and avoided any form of authority. He stole from shops and sold on the goods for food, and he also robbed people on the streets, again to buy food. He took drugs and alcohol to numb the pain he felt when he thought about his life and although he did contemplate suicide, he could never work out why he did not kill himself. Why he continued to lead such a miserable life was a question he could not answer. Eventually he found himself serving a juvenile sentence. A sign of how miserable his life had been on the streets was the fact that he enjoyed being in custody, where he was guaranteed a bed, food, warmth, shelter and the opportunity to mix with people his own age. I always felt he was offering minimal information about his life on the streets and believed there was a more sinister story to be told. Maybe one day he would tell me, but this moment in time was not it.

Vernon survived on the streets because his genes triggered his natural instincts to survive and he responded the only way he knew how. Explaining to Vernon why our natural instincts to survive 'kick in', even when our lives are in despair, was not a way of offering him an excuse for his behaviour but a way of explaining how we all have the same natural instincts to survive.

I condemn all forms of criminal activity but as I have previously mentioned in chapter 3, when working with someone like Vernon in order to support them I have to be emphatic. Vernon was a child on the street alone and hungry, he responded the only way he knew how and now I believe lived with the consequences of his actions.

Vernon left the young offenders' institute and started a basic college course in music technology but it was not long before he returned to a custodial sentence. I did notice a change in him as he showed some remorse, but because so many negative seeds had been sown in his early life, I knew it would take a long time and a lot of hard work on his behalf before he would see the error of his ways. He had given up the idea of being a rap star as he realized he could not rap, but he did turn his hand to poetry and often had his worked published in the prison newsletter. As he continued to drift in and out of prison sentences I could not help thinking that maybe prison remained his only safe haven.

Self-preservation

Self-preservation is our guardian. This will explain a newborn baby's ability to suck milk from its mother. Even when it has not been nurtured to do so, the baby has the need to seek nourishment. The baby is using its natural instincts to survive. Later in life the child will learn how to use utensils to eat, and they will learn what I call 'appropriate behaviour', namely the behaviour they need to be part of society.

Prisons are full of people who are lacking in appropriate behaviour – indeed they display 'offending behaviour'. Failure to learn appropriate behaviour such as communication skills could leave an individual struggling to exist within the set boundaries of society. Our natural instinct to survive will remain, regardless of the level of appropriate behaviour we learn, which implies that we still need to eat and have somewhere to live. However, our ability to earn the money we need to live comfortably will be affected by our level of appropriate behaviour. Failure to have learnt appropriate behaviour does not give us an excuse to behave as we wish but it does explain some offending behaviour.

The reproductive instinct can cause difficulties for an individual lacking in appropriate behaviour. They may perceive sex and the pleasure they receive from it as the one and only objective. They find it difficult to express emotion or behaviour associated with love and affection, as they do not appreciate the responsibilities and reason for sex, the responsibilities of parenting, caring for family members or loyalties.

In this chapter I have discussed our natural instinct to survive and the influence of nature versus nurture debate. In the next chapter I want to look at the specific needs we all have in our lives, the need for nourishment, a safe environment to live, relationships, healthy self-esteem and ultimately self-fulfilment.

R U listenin'?

- Survival is a basic instinct.
- Many of our decisions in life are based on our need to survive.
- Our behaviour is not a pre-set disposition.
- Our environment and relationships can influence our behaviour.

Chapter 6

Offending Behaviour

 I admit to being challenging in my group work both in prisons and on the outside. I find it gets to people's true inner feelings quickly and makes for good group discussions. It is an acquired skill and not one I would recommend to anyone working in a similar field without having years of experience. Challenging people's beliefs has the potential to cause very dangerous situations if the situation is not facilitated correctly.

For me, personally, the most annoying response I get when challenging a person who has committed a crime is the expression 'they were asking for it'. By this they mean that someone had a large wallet stuffed in their back pocket for all to see, or they put their mobile phone on a table in a pub while they had a drink, left a bedroom window open, left their bicycle unlocked, left their laptop on the seat of their car or simply looked at someone inquisitively. No one asks to be a victim of crime. It is a decision taken by a human being to break what is otherwise seen as moral code of human behaviour.

What I want to focus on in this chapter is our ability to satisfy levels of need. By 'need', I mean the need to have food, shelter, relationships and love. These are needs which are not to be confused with 'wants'. Each time you switch your television on or browse through a glossy magazine your natural human needs are being bombarded by clever advertising suggesting that you are in some way inadequate or not treating yourself appropriately. If we believe all the advertisements, we are in a real mess and we thank God for all those products advertised that are going to make us the human being we really want to be. That is, providing we eat a particular brand of yoghurt, wash our hair with a vitamin-rich shampoo, eat the healthy-option breakfast cereal, brush our teeth with whiter-than-white toothpaste or moisturize our skin with a specially formulated cream – the list goes on for ever.

If we understand why we have natural needs to fulfil, we are more likely to take control of our life. We know that advertisements are designed to exploit our natural needs, but it is important to remember that the code of practice in advertising is to make a need into a 'want'. I need a pair of jeans to keep me warm but after watching the designer jeans advertisement I may decide I don't need just a pair of jeans, I 'want' a pair of designer jeans. Not only will they keep me warm, but I will also be attractive to the opposite sex. Once we understand our needs, we are then in a position to appreciate why we feel the way we do and why we all have similar worries and woes.

Moral code

The psychologist Abraham Maslow did not accept that lying, cheating, stealing and murder were part of human nature. He suggested that such behaviours were the actions of people who had been deprived of role models to teach them appropriate behaviour. These people maintain their basic human instincts to survive but lack the appropriate behaviour needed to control them.

Maslow identified the basic human needs in 'levels'. He believed there were four levels of need that had to be satisfied before a person could contemplate a fifth level where they are able to recognize their true potential. He called them his 'hierarchy of needs'. One moved up a level as needs were met.

- The most basic level is the need to function.

- The second is the need for safety.

- The third is the desire for love.

- The fourth is a quest for esteem.

- The final level is that of self-actualization and the search for inner peace.

Level 1: Physiological needs. The body craves food, liquid, sleep, oxygen, sex, freedom of movement and a moderate temperature.

Level 2: Safety and security. We need a certain level of physical comfort while at the same time looking for predictability and certainty. We want to know that we are guaranteed our next meal and our guardians will be there to tuck us up in bed at night.

Level 3: Love and belonging. At this level we are looking to give and receive love. We need to feel wanted and to be able to please others. This is not to be confused with esteem. Having three lovers may be more of an 'esteem-injec-tion' than a sharing of love.

Level 4: Self-esteem. This is a level of competence in carrying out a specific task, complemented with the attention and recognition of others.

Level 5: Self-actualization. You have met your needs for the time being at levels 1–4 and desire to reach your full potential. This can be interpreted by the individual in many forms: when taking decisions about personal growth, problem solving personal and professional issues, the development of a moral code, acceptance of others and their beliefs. All may be used in a quest for knowledge, peace, self-fulfilment and maturity. It is important to note that this level, as with all levels, is not age-related.

I am not suggesting Maslow had the perfect answer. He does, however, put things into a perspective that we are able to recognize and relate to. Satisfying our needs is healthy – failure to do so can have a direct impact on our well-being.

We all have the same set of basic needs. How we address our needs may be different but they are as fulfilling to us as the next person.

Anyone can sit down and ponder the meaning of life, but what Maslow is suggesting is that this can only truly be done when someone has fulfilled their other needs. For example, a person cannot attend a masters course at university if they have not achieved their GCSEs, 'A' levels and degree, simply because they would not have the required knowledge.

Exercise 6: Offending behaviour

Group and individual exercise; see Chapter 15.

Joe: Fraud – four years

There is no exact science for determining when and how we meet our needs. But I will make an attempt with Joe's case study to identify times in his life when I believe he was addressing specific needs.

Joe was raised in London on a council estate and was the youngest of nine brothers and sisters. His father drifted in and out of casual work and was never able to maintain a steady income. Joe knew what it was like to be hungry everyday and come home to a cold house. (Level 1, Physiological needs)

At age 11, he passed his school exams and was offered a scholarship to his local grammar school. His brothers and sisters were now of working age and financially the family were comfortable. Joe had a good circle of friends on the council estate and played football for the local youth club. (Level 2, Safety and security)

Joe entered a competition arranged by a bank, and for this he designed a series of posters and developed a business plan. He won first prize and was awarded a sponsorship by the bank to pay for additional tuition after school hours. They guaranteed him a position with the bank when he left school providing he achieved the necessary grades in his exams. He was able to appreciate the support his brothers, sisters and friends from school offered him. He started dating and began to look long-term to his career and the material luxuries he could earn with hard work. (Level 3, Love and belonging)

Joe started working for the bank in a job he enjoyed, his career was taking off and he could not have wished for anything more. He was well regarded by his co-workers, had a good social life, looked after himself physically and moved into his own flat. (Level 4, Esteem needs). At work he met and fell head over heels in love with a woman ten years his senior. She persuaded him that the only way to truly satisfy his needs was with money. She had a plan to steal money from the bank and needed Joe's help. Love is a need that we all seek and Joe was no different. He tried to defraud the bank, was caught and subsequently sentenced.

Joe was a 'good lad' (a person trusted by other prisoners). He had a job in the library checking books in and out and he had a talent for recommending books to other prisoners without embarrassing them about their level of literacy. I remember talking to him about money and how it had affected his career. I recall using the classic quote, 'money is not everything', and while Joe agreed he added, 'Money is not everything, but it is a big chunk of everything.' In other words, money can play a big part in helping us to achieve our needs, which I had to agree with.

As we talked about his life to date, the people he had disappointed, including himself, and the lessons he had learnt from his prison sentence, I began to feel that he had learnt the importance of a moral code. He was able to view all aspects of his life with a mature approach. He displayed creativity, spontaneity and problem-solving skills when talking about how he would get his career and social life back on track when released from prison. Growing up in a multicultural environment, and his time spent in prison, had taught him not to have prejudice and to separate fact from fiction. Had we not been having the conversation in a prison I would have suggested he was content with his life and had recognized Level 5, Self-actualization.

However, we were in a prison environment and my experience of prisoners has made me a healthy sceptic. I knew that the true test of what individuals learn about themselves from a prison sentence could only truly be expressed back in society. On this occasion, I like to think my scepticism was ill-founded.

Do we experience all levels?

You may be familiar with the expression 'spoilt brat', often used to describe a person who is privileged and does not appreciate it. Having doting parents who catered for their every need may have inadvertently prevented them from appreciating their privileged lifestyle.

The same person who does not appreciate an affluent upbringing and who takes everything for granted, may experience difficulties in their life if they are suddenly faced with poverty. Alternatively, the same people may put up with all kinds of hardship, danger and loneliness later on in life in order to gain a sense of worth.

Understanding the needs Maslow identified and how we fulfil them will have a direct impact on the way we feel about ourselves. The fact that you are reading this book could place you in the self-actualization level (i.e. your basic needs have been met and you are now achieving self-fulfilment). On the other hand, by reading this book you may realize that your basic needs have not been met and you may need to take a step back and address them.

Gavin: Taking without the owner's consent, car theft (TWOC) – three months

Gavin came from the sort of background a lot of people dream of. He was raised in a financially-secure environment and he wanted for nothing. He received the best education money could buy and attended one of the country's top private schools before being arrested on several occasions for TWOC.

When I met Gavin he was like a 'fish out of water' – his upbringing had not prepared him for life in prison. To the outside world he had everything materially but this did not mean that all his needs had been addressed. When he was growing up he did not see much of his parents because they were always working and this had left him emotionally stranded, desperately seeking love and a sense of belonging. The attention he received from the police, social services and people working in similar roles to me when he was caught offending, was a substitute for the emotional needs he could not fill.

His parents' immediate reaction to his sentence was to ensure he had everything he needed materially and financially while in prison. They failed to appreciate that in prison you earn your privileges and that in Gavin's case he had to obey Her Majesty's Young Offenders' Institute (HMYOI) rules and regulations. The following is a list of kit Gavin would have received:

1 pair of jeans	7 pairs of socks
1 pair of PE shorts	1 pair of pyjamas
2 tracksuit bottoms	2 towels
2 tracksuit tops	1 flannel
2 T-shirts	1 kit bag
2 PE vests	1 shirt
7 pairs of boxer shorts	

In addition to the clothing:

1 CD player
Religious articles
Plain wedding band

Any other items would require permission from the governor.

Gavin would be allowed two visits a month by family and friends and would also be allowed to purchase a selection of items from the canteen list (i.e. toiletries, confectionery and stamps). The canteen would give him the opportunity of spending £10 per week of his private savings, money he may have earned from attending education or having a job. Gavin's cell would contain a fixed toilet and sink, one table, cupboard, locker and bed. (Although I worked with Gavin many years ago, I have based all of the above on today's Standard Level privileges. On a Basic Level they would receive less, and on an Enhanced Level they would receive more.)

When Gavin's parents read through the prison regulations, it brought home to them the reality of their son's predicament and they immediately feared for his ability to deal with the emotional and physical environment he found himself in. By working with Gavin and his parents I was able to quash some of their fears about the harsh reality of prison life, and help them realize that to all intents and purposes, Gavin was well looked after by the staff and in a safe environment. I also got his parents to concentrate on what they could offer their son emotionally – not materially or financially. It was a difficult time for the whole family – they all served the sentence together learning the old adage 'you do not appreciate what you have got until you no longer have it'. Gavin had a difficult time in prison but I believe he left to return to his privileged life-style with a greater understanding of himself and his needs.

He wrote to me at a later date explaining how his prison experience had changed his life. He noted how it had made him appreciate his family and many of life's simple pleasures and as I read the letters I realized he was consciously aware of levels of need, possible for first time in his life. An interesting footnote to Gavin's case study was a letter I received from his parents which was almost identical to Gavin's letter. They thanked me for my support and commented on how the experience had changed their lives by making them appreciate what a wonderful son they had.

Meeting your needs

If you believe all the glossy advertisements in the Sunday supplements suggesting that a career with a steady income, a loving partner, two children, a cat, a dog and a cottage in a clean, safe environment would fulfil your needs, then those things are probably right for you. Why? Because the above probably meets the majority of most people's needs. This is not to say they will not be without problems. Sadly, trying to achieve them could possibly lead to divorce, huge debts and emotional turmoil for families.

For example, if we want the cottage in the country then we need to work hard and save our pennies, but if we do not earn enough to buy a cottage then we need to look at what we can realistically afford. Holding a bank up for the money is inappropriate behaviour and does not fulfil any needs. Constantly beating yourself up because you cannot afford a cottage is also inappropriate behaviour and fulfils no needs.

We can fulfil our needs – we simply need to adjust our sights and get real. We should not take all the advertising to heart. Comparing our lives with those of others is a way of setting goals but is detrimental if we set unrealistic goals that attack our well-being. The needs you have are perfectly natural, but you need to start being realistic about the degree to which you can meet your needs and start planning how, and when, you aim to achieve them. Chapter 14 will help you plan your objectives.

Addressing your needs is not a sin but is, in fact, perfectly natural. Preventing yourself from addressing your basic needs is unnatural and will lead you down a path of confusion and dissatisfaction with your life. Most of us invest a lot of our time 'discussing' with ourselves how we are feeling, where we are at in our lives and where we would like to be. We 'talk' around our needs and how they have been filled or not, and this process is often referred to as 'self-talk'. The majority of people I work with are not aware of this process and some even consider themselves crazy for doing it. Mastering the art of self-talk will change your life and in the next chapter we will explore the power of our self-talk and its ability to enhance our well-being or destroy it.

R U listenin'?

- We all have the same basic needs.
- We learn appropriate behaviour.
- Offending behaviour is not part of our make-up.
- Recognizing your needs will breed contentment.
- Be realistic when addressing your needs.

Chapter 7

Segregation

 I received a request to interview a prisoner aged 64. The prisoner in question was known as Buddha because of his slow, methodical approach to prison life and his round physique. He would soon be leaving the prison and required advice on jobs. When I read his file I noted that he was a regular visitor to the segregation unit and when I asked his wing officer why he spent so much time in the segregation unit, he said, 'It was by choice – it was his retreat.' When I met with Buddha, or to give him his real name, Tom, I asked why he appeared to enjoy spending time in segregation. He listed the following reasons:

- It's my cocoon.
- It gets you away from all the nastiness in the prison.
- Gives you time to think.
- A chance to talk some sense.
- Have a word with yourself.
- Be at peace.
- Talk to my best mate – me.
- Get a good night's sleep.

By the time Buddha (Tom) had finished listing his reasons for going to the unit I had decided that this was a place I would like to visit occasionally! I wondered why the segregation unit was used as a punishment if it was such a comfortable place to be.

The words that stuck in my mind from our conversation were 'have a word with yourself'. Communication is a skill. Over the years, in the course of my work, I have studied the subject of communication skills and gained a variety of qualifications in connection with personal development. However, communicating with ourselves, which is probably the most important form of communication in our lives, is a skill rarely taught in schools or colleges.

Tom had obviously discovered the secret of talking to himself in a constructive way. I guess the assumption of the prison authorities is that most people have this skill, and placing them in segregation offers them the opportunity to reflect on their actions and see the error of their ways. In my experience, a lot of people do not have this skill and left in their own company with nothing to occupy their minds leads them to having one-way conversations, which, depending on their state of mind, can sometimes be destructive.

In this chapter I want to explore the idea that we all 'have a word with ourselves' occasionally. Depending on how beneficial or destructive our conversations are, we can influence how we lead our lives. By understanding the processes we are experiencing (or to be more specific, the conversations we have with ourselves), we can take control of the situation and ensure we have well balanced and constructive conversations. Tom mentioned that he talked to his 'best mate'. The idea of making ourselves our own best mate is something I have tried to teach others and a concept I promote.

Why do we segregate prisoners?

When a decision is taken to escort a prisoner to the segregation unit, the corridors are cleared and prison officers escort the individual. In some cases there is a need to restrain the individual and assist them in their journey. However, not all prisoners in the segregation unit are there for failing to obey prison rules; some actually request to be placed in segregation.

The segregation unit within a prison is used to hold prisoners who are either a threat to themselves or others, or for those who would benefit from some time in their own company away from the general population. The decision to segregate is a last resort. Other options may be offered including closer supervision, a transfer to another wing or even to another prison.

The segregation cell can be the same as a normal cell, or it may have cardboard furniture. The extreme is a cell with a mattress, no fixtures or fittings and closed-circuit TV for close supervision by trained staff. There is an exercise yard attached to the unit where the prisoner will have an opportunity to exercise in the open air.

While they are in segregation prisoners are observed in their cell at regular times. Depending on their condition, observation times can vary from 5- to

30-minute intervals. When a prisoner leaves the segregation unit, their behaviour is detailed in a report, which accompanies them wherever they are sent.

The staff that work in the segregation unit are charged with the responsibility of ensuring a positive atmosphere and building up a constructive and supportive relationship with those held in their care.

The reasons why someone may choose to be sent to the segregation unit are:

- A prisoner may request a move to a segregation unit for their own safety.
- An inability by the individual to cope on a wing.
- Stress.
- Bereavement.
- Home circumstances.

I believe you may send yourself into 'segregation' in your own mind for the same reasons. You feel safe when you are away from all of life's worries and woes. However, once you book into your own segregation unit, do you use the time to understand yourself or criticize yourself?

Exercise 7: Segregation
Group exercise; see Chapter 15.

Life happens

In Great Britain in 2007 approximately 80,000 people were serving a custodial sentence from a population of approximately 57 million. Not all these people were murderers or violent individuals: the majority were petty criminals. If we are to believe the media, our country is awash with violence – but it is not. However, we all know that crime sells newspapers and gets the ratings on television. Our mind has the same tendency to highlight dramatic times in our life. The normal run-of-the-mill days we have for the majority of our life, do not make the headlines.

As a result of a situation in which we have been involved, our belief about what may happen to us can often be exaggerated. There is a good reason for this cautious approach: our survival may depend upon it. We could lose our job if we are consistently late for work and so our concern ensures we are punctual. However, far too often, people are overly concerned about a potential situation and talk themselves into a state of unnecessary concern.

If you lose your wallet, do you learn to be more careful next time when placing it in your back pocket, or do you see it as another sign of your incompetence? Perhaps you use the event as another emotional experience to call upon when you are beating yourself up about your incompetences. You may recall other times in your life when you have been incompetent and this starts a chain reaction of negative thoughts. Feeling incompetent is understandable. However, linking other events and talking yourself down is not. How you cope with criticism from yourself is crucial. Remember, you are the person who knows everything about you. You know all your weaknesses and what to say or do to trigger off attacks on your self-esteem.

The process of 'having a word with yourself' is often referred to as 'self-talk' and everyone on the planet self-talks: it is impossible not to. How I distinguish self-talk from everyday thought-processing is as follows:

While walking around the supermarket, considering what to have for my dinner, I narrow down my choice to pizza or roast chicken. How I make my final decision will be based on a number of influences and needs, including the cost of the products, my personal preference, convenience of cooking and sometimes even the weather may influence my decision. This is known as processing information – it is not self-talk. However, remembering what your friend said about your inability to cook due to your incompetence with food makes you feel inadequate. You may then begin a conversation with yourself about all the other areas in your life where you feel inadequate and this affects your mood – this is self-talk. You have entered into a conversation with yourself that will affect your emotional well-being.

Jacob: Violence – two years

I asked Jacob to write a piece of work for me about a situation when his self-talk dictated his actions and he produced the following:

> One day while walking to work I was thinking about what I should buy for lunch. If I went to the supermarket, there would be a bigger selection of sandwiches and it would be cheaper than the local shop. However, this would involve a detour, which could make me late, and I had already received a warning about my time-keeping. I decided to walk faster, not stop off for a newspaper and go straight to the supermarket, confident that I would not be late.
>
> As I rushed to the supermarket I began to get a little anxious as to whether I had made the right decision. I began to recall a time when I was younger and was out shopping with my mother. As we left the supermarket we were stopped by two boys (younger and smaller than me) who snatched my mother's bag and ran away with it. I did nothing to help her – I just stood

there and cried. When I got home my father called me a coward and sent me to my room.

When I reached the supermarket I found that there was a large queue. I knew this would make me late and my self-talk started getting the better of me. I began to criticize myself for being a coward all those years ago and I started feeling vulnerable to attack and wished I was tooled up [carrying a weapon]. I imagined what I would do if someone tried to snatch the handbag of the old lady in front of me in the queue: I would smash their faces in. Within a matter of seconds I had gone from a carefree person on his way to work, to a raging bull ready to destroy anyone who stood in my way.

Having to queue at the supermarket added to my anxiety and my self-talk kept reminding me what an idiot I had been for coming in the first place – I should have gone straight to work. I arrived at work late and angry with myself, not just because I was late, but for so many other times in my life when I should have stood up for myself and did not. My boss had a go at me for being late and I exploded! I told him where to stick his job and threatened to batter him if I ever saw him on the street. I had started the morning strolling to work to a job I enjoyed, but within an hour I was sacked and back to struggling to find money to pay the bills. Worse still, I had let my family down.

This is what some people refer to as a bad day. It's what I have learnt to call a 'chokey [segregation unit] day'. Whenever I recall events like this and realize how I have screwed my life up and wasted opportunities, I get angry and lash out at anyone who looks at me the wrong way, and I end up being in the chokey. Once I am in the chokey, my self-talk runs riot, recalling events from my past when I was weak and afraid. I dread going to the chokey because it's a place where all my nightmares wait to haunt me.

Guilt

Jacob was experiencing guilt from a past experience. He believed he had been a coward. This was an irrational belief. If Jacob had been the person who had stolen the handbag and was now experiencing guilt, then this would have been a rational guilt based on his moral code. However, his irrational guilt was based on a traumatic event to which he had responded emotionally.

Jacob's reaction was one of aggression but some people might have reacted passively. Both reactions are counter-productive. A middle ground must be achieved, as shown in the following diagram.

GUILT

Rational guilt based on our moral code	Diplomacy	Irrational guilt based on a traumatic experience

A person who is experiencing rational guilt has the opportunity to give themselves up, or right their wrong by showing remorse and offering to make amends. A person who has irrational guilt will experience difficulty with this as they have nothing to be guilty about. Jacob had been traumatized by an event he now felt guilty about and he used it to attack his self-esteem.

Can you recall an event you struggle to address, such as 20 years ago you sat in the wrong classroom in school for half an hour before you realized. Everyone laughed at you and pulled your leg about it for weeks after the event. You still feel foolish about the event today and often recall it to back up your belief about your stupidity whenever you do something wrong. If you have experienced a traumatic event that you still feel guilty about, and that guilt is irrational, then you will struggle to resolve it. Let's introduce diplomacy and positive self-talk into Jacob's predicament.

- I understand why my father called me a coward.

- My father's approval was important to me – however he should have known better than to criticize me.

- I was a young boy at the time.

- If I had a son and the same happened to him, I would not call him a coward. I would hug him and explain why people behave in such a way.

- The bag my mother was carrying had only a few pounds in it. Money is not everything.

- I have a responsible job, a family and a mortgage to meet every month, a coward would not take on such responsibilities.

- Anyone who has to steal handbags should be pitied.

- Sad people with no morals are not going to ruin my life.

- I have too many fond memories of time spent with my mother to let this one upset me.

- Being diplomatic makes my self-talk a pleasant experience.

Sometimes people ask me how I can work with some of the people I do knowing the crimes they have committed. The answer is I have empathy – the ability to try to understand where they are coming from. This helps me to understand why they behave the way they do.

Keith: Actual Bodily Harm (ABH) – three years

Keith launched an unprovoked attack on a taxi driver. When I questioned his motive it became obvious that it was racially-based. He talked at length about his racist beliefs and over time I realized he came from a racist family, who had nurtured these beliefs. However, being in prison, Keith had to share with people from a variety of backgrounds – he had no choice. I encouraged him to speak to these people and to try to understand why their beliefs were different to his. This helped him recognize that his racist beliefs were unfounded, and he learnt to appreciate why other people hold different beliefs and follow different customs. Keith learnt empathy and he also introduced diplomacy into his self-talk. This helped him to understand himself and deal with his own emotional turmoil. The more open-minded we are towards others, the more open-minded we are to ourselves.

We can do the same with our emotions by trying to understand where they are coming from and why they visit us at certain moments in our life. Remember, emotions such as anxiety, guilt, inferior feelings and jealousy visit us when we are feeling low. If you are prepared for such events you can deal with them in a constructive way and be able to raise your mood instead of letting yourself wallow in self-pity. Try using empathy and diplomacy when you self-talk and make it a constructive conversation, not an attack on your well-being.

Any form of segregation is a scary place if you are your own worst company. When I refer to segregation I do not necessarily mean being locked in a room alone. You can segregate yourself in the company of others, while walking around a supermarket or driving a car. I refer to the process of being alone with your thoughts and emotions. In your own company you may have a tendency to fester on past memories that upset you. Holding onto exaggerated beliefs and drawing upon them whenever we are placed in similar predicaments is something we are all guilty of. These exaggerated beliefs become dangerous and begin to chip away at our self-esteem. We need to challenge our beliefs and change our way of interpreting a situation. This is not easy, but it is also not impossible. We need to learn to be a diplomat when addressing ourselves about given situations and how they may impact on our life.

I do not suggest you debate every thought and emotion you experience. What I do suggest, however, is that you learn to be calm and diplomatic. You need to appreciate the speed at which you can talk yourself into a state of anxiety. I refrain from using the word 'depression' because depression can be a serious illness and the word is bandied about far too often. What you may be guilty of is believing that external events are causing your anxiety, when in reality, it is your perception of the event. Events, over which we have no control, happen – that's life. How we perceive and deal with the event can be controlled with positive and supportive self-talk. Each event is an opportunity to boost our positive self-talk enabling us to cope with other experiences and beliefs in our life.

Monitor your language

Losing your wallet is an inconvenience, but not life-threatening. Missing your train is inconvenient, but not a disaster. The stronger your language in describing your perception of an event, the greater it will impact on your well-being. If you believe that dropping an armful of paper in the office is a catastrophe, what would you consider a bump in your car to be – the end of the world? It's no surprise then that some people struggle to deal with situations when their self-talk blows all events out of proportion.

Look at the areas in your life affected by self-talk:

- Your emotions.
- Behaviour.
- Self-esteem.
- Relationships.
- Health.

Catching yourself in self-talk can be done spontaneously or by looking at your watch each hour and noting if you are in self-talk. You can register what the conversation is about and whether you are being positive or negative in your talk. You can write down the event you are debating and what you believe the eventual outcome will be. Do this each time you catch yourself in self-talk. On occasions your worst fears may be recognized, but in the majority of cases you will have fretted over nothing because you will have exaggerated your self-talk and given yourself unnecessary anxiety.

Detailing Jacob's self-talk helped him realize how often he attached emotionally-upsetting memories onto present-day concerns, and this process ultimately blew everything out of proportion. It is a useful exercise to establish the number of negative emotional memories you have in your own 'library' and you may be surprised to find that the number you use to back up your negative self-talk is actually quite small. However, the number of times you draw on these negative emotions can be phenomenal.

To enhance your positive self-talk take a concern you have, think of the advice you would give a friend who asked you for advice on the same matter and give yourself the same positive, supportive advice. Be prepared for times when you might lapse into negative self-talk. It is best to explore where your negative self-talk stems from when you are in a positive state of mind. Addressing your negative self-talk when you are feeling negative will, at best, be difficult but at worst will add to your anxiety.

Identifying why we hold onto negative emotions and where they come from will be addressed in the next chapter when we look at the rehabilitation programme used in prisons to prepare prisoners for a life 'on the out'.

If you're wondering if Tom got a job on release – he did. He worked in his local supermarket stacking shelves and when I met him one day I enquired if he was happy with his life and if he missed the segregation unit. He told me he was content, which is better than being happy. His new segregation unit was a park bench where he would sit and 'have a word with himself', and yes, he was still his own best friend although he did have the occasional falling out!

R U listenin'?

- Give yourself the same advice you would offer others.
- Catch yourself being negative or positive.
- Be a diplomat.
- Have empathy.
- Don't fester on the problem – address it.
- Be aware of rational and irrational guilt.

Chapter 8

Institutionalization

 One day I met a prisoner walking along one of the prison corridors on his way to a workshop. He had recently been released and so I was surprised to see him return so quickly. I asked him what had gone wrong and he explained that when he was released from prison he was determined to stay off the alcohol and lead a healthy life. Shortly after his release from prison, he went to a supermarket to buy some cheese and he was faced with over 50 varieties. After spending an hour trying to decide which cheese to buy, he felt so stressed that he bought a bottle of cider, and his spiral back to prison began.

When I see a prisoner returning to prison after committing another offence I never know who is more disappointed, the prisoner or myself. The acceptance of their fate due to the life they lead is a crime in itself. I can never accept this philosophy, as I believe we all have the ability to control our own destinies. It could be that I have got it wrong and maybe these people are controlling their own destinies by leading lives they know will return them to the prison environment.

Is it true that some people are happy to be in a prison? No, they are not happy. However, some people prefer to be in prison where they know the regime and how it works, as opposed to a life outside the boundaries of a disciplined environment where they are stressed and frightened, not knowing what challenges tomorrow may bring. They fear the pressure of everyday life and are unable to make decisions. They prefer the option of other people making decisions for them because this allows them the luxury of being able to blame others for any inadequacies in their life.

Paul's diary

A page from Paul's personal prison diary reads:

> I was awake and ready for breakfast before the screws had opened my cell
> door. Breakfast was the usual scran [food] with extra sausages – the sell-by
> dates must have been up. I knew a lad on our landing was not going to his
> art class in the education block because he had a solicitor's visit. I managed
> to blag [convince] the screws that I be allowed to take his place in the art
> class. In the class Miss let me have a go at some pottery – I made meself an
> ashtray. Waste of time, she wouldn't let me take it back to me cell. It would
> go to reception. [When a prisoner enters a prison all his goods are stored in
> reception for safekeeping.] I could collect it on release. What use is that?
> It's two years before I'm released. She's not a bad one though – she gave
> me some writing paper for letters. Went back to the wing for lunch – not
> bad had some sort of a rice dish. Had bang up [locked in the cell] for a
> couple of hours, Mr Harris our wing officer was in a good mood – took
> five of us up to the gym for two hours. Had a good workout and a nice hot
> shower afterwards. Someone had left their shower gel in the changing
> rooms so I also gained a full bottle of shower gel, which I swapped for
> some tobacco on the way back to the wing. Had a couple more hours bang
> up then supper. It was slops [poor food] but after me workout I was
> starving and ate it anyway. Banged up again until association when we
> were allowed to watch TV – had a couple of games of pool and shared me
> tobacco with Steve. He gave me a couple of books to read. Back in the cell
> before lights out I had a read of the books – both are murder mysteries, did
> me diary entry, not a bad day today.

Reading into Paul's diary one realizes the extent to which prisoners are controlled to the point of requiring permission from others to lead their lives. Paul
will experience this daily routine for at least four years before he is released and
expected to take responsibility for himself.

These are just some of the many reasons why people like Paul spend their
lives in and out of prison:

- Many prisoners will have spent time in care as a child, which is an
  experience that may affect their ability to live on their own or to
  develop independence.

- Most prisoners have poor basic skills, which impacts on their ability
  to cope with finances, fill in forms, access services and stand up for
  their rights.

- As a result of truancy or exclusion from school, many will have low levels of self-esteem.

- Many prisoners have little or no experience of employment and the disciplines necessary to sustain a job.

All the above lend a person to being institutionalized.

One of the reasons people tell me they are relaxed in prison is the knowledge that everyone else around them has broken the law. Outside the prison they are looked down upon but inside prison they are an equal. They can be themselves and talk openly about what they have done or plan to do. Prisons are seen as breeding grounds for crime where prisoners exchange ideas about criminal activities. Personally, I would take any information offered by a person serving a custodial sentence with a pinch of salt. What they will learn is institutionalization. A custodial sentence takes away an individual's freedom and relieves them of their responsibilities. They become dependent on others to make decisions for them and lose, or never learn, the necessary skills to lead a full and independent life.

Exercise 8: Institutionalization

Group and individual exercise; see Chapter 15.

Resettlement

'Resettlement' is a prison initiative, which is designed to support prisoners who are nearing the end of their sentence and help them make the transition from prison to a life of freedom. The key area addressed is independence. The programme prepares them for the many obstacles they will encounter on release and concentrates on the areas of finance, living accommodation, relationships with family and friends, personal responsibilities, employment and health. The programme may involve home visits (as the name suggests, a visit to the individual's home address for a few days) but they will be trusted to return to prison on an agreed date. The individual is responsible for attending the programme and is required to participate in all activities and assessments. They will need to display a positive approach to their release and, most importantly, prove they are not institutionalized and are able to cope on their own. Their participation in the programme will be taken into account when they go before the parole board.

Resettlement group: variety of offences and sentences

I entered the prison one morning expecting to take a new group for a new, one-week personal-development course I had written. When I reached the education wing I was informed that the tutor who was timetabled to take the resettlement group had phoned in sick. The group had to be taken and so I was asked to help out. For obvious reasons I had no resettlement work prepared and so I decided I would improvise some of my own work to tie in with what the group were already doing. This was not the first time this had happened to me. I have delivered sessions in every subject and so I can always manage to improvise something and everyone is usually happy. I never refuse because it would be unfair on the prisoners who would have to stay in their cells. My style of delivery is based on interaction and fun, which always goes down well with people from all walks of life. When I walked into the training room I recognized the majority of faces, because they had attended my sessions, and so the work I thought I could use was no longer an option. Before I opened my mouth to admit to being in a bit of a pickle, one of the men asked if they could go next door to the art room to finish off their projects. This was the answer to my predicament. As always, I took credit for the idea, implying that I was just about to make the very same suggestion. We informed the officers on duty and were able to move the class with little effort. I realized this was turning out to be a good day – I would leave the men to their own devices and get on with my own work.

Before I had a chance to settle down, I was asked for equipment from the storeroom and then tools from the shadow cases. (These are glass cases on the wall where tools hang with their silhouette behind, which highlights any tools removed, and makes it easy to see if there are any missing tools at the end of the session.) I have an art qualification and so I was able to offer advice on individual artwork, but what did surprise me was the constant bombardment of questions. If I was not being asked about what type of pencil, pastel, oil, water-colour, felt tip or crayon to use I was being asked about composition, presentation, perspective, texture and scale. Then, my opinion would be required on the quality of the artwork and I began to feel that no one would take any decisions for themselves. Although I would never criticize anyone's work as I believe effort, not necessarily quality, is the important ingredient, I fully appreciated how important my opinion was to them and how devastating the effect could be if I was negative about someone's work.

What I thought was going to be an easy day turned out to be exhausting. I appreciated that people wanted to produce a good piece of work but it was their inability to take a decision that amazed me. I reminded myself that this was the resettlement group and that these men would be released shortly and be expected to make all kinds of decisions about their lives on a daily basis. I just hoped they would not struggle to take decisions in the same way they had in the art session. The men had to make a request for every piece of equipment which, in turn, I was responsible for noting and in some cases identifying with tags. I had to count out every piece of equipment and count it all back in at the end of the session before anyone was allowed to leave the room. I appreciate the role prisons play in taking away people's ability to make decisions and so it is no surprise to me that people become institutionalized in prison – it is the best place for it.

How do we become institutionalized?

People who are institutionalized will identify with other people who are in the same situation. They will support each other's belief that there is nothing they can do to change their predicament. For some, institutionalization is a choice they knowingly make. Their decision could be based on financial benefits (i.e. a relationship that can offer financial security providing they obey the rules set out by the person with the money). They are willing victims of a lifestyle that may lead them to become institutionalized. These are some of the factors which may lead us to become institutionalized:

- As children we are easily misunderstood by those in charge. A child with an opinion may be seen as a naughty child. We may be disciplined to believe our opinion is not as important as that of others who know better. Such beliefs can be carried into adulthood and never really challenged, which can prepare us for a life of institutionalization.

- Following the instructions or advice of others often results in us being looked upon favourably and so we continue to do as we are told.

- Some schools (not all) are ideal breeding grounds for implementing the seeds of institutionalization. What is seen as discipline could be responsible for suppressing confidence and sowing the seeds of institutionalization.

- We may have learnt that institutionalization is an opportunity to dip in and out of our responsibilities.

You may be institutionalized if you can relate to the following:

- Do you shy away from responsibility?

- Is your decision-making easily swayed?

- Do you prefer to let others make decisions for you?

- Do you feel you are in the wrong job or relationship and unable to break free from the constraints?

- Do you lack ambition?

- Do you complain about your lifestyle?

What are the benefits of independence?

- Being able to be the real you.

- Letting others know what you really want from your life.

- Increasing the chances of meeting the people who can help to give you the life you want.

- Having a greater understanding of yourself, which in turn will make you more understanding of others.

- Enjoying new responsibilities in your life.

Independence allows you to take control of your own destiny and disempowers others who may have been taking your decision-making away from you.

A person who does not drive a car and depends on others for lifts knows they would benefit from learning to drive, because it would enhance their quality of life. They would be able to go whenever, and wherever, they wanted to go but instead they rely on other people's goodwill. Ultimately they may be missing out on new experiences in their life.

An independent person who is accustomed to taking control of a situation would take driving lessons, even if they could not afford to buy a car. They may believe that having a licence may encourage them to save for a car or that it would increase their chances of future employment. Whatever they believe, they are taking control of their destiny. They can see only the benefits of having a driving licence and do not place barriers in their way.

The following diagram lists beliefs held by an institutionalized and an independent person. Which category do you fit into?

Institutionalized	Independent
There is nothing I can do.	Let's look at the alternatives.
That's just the way I am.	I can choose a different approach.
She makes me so mad.	I control my own feelings.
They won't allow that.	I can present it well and persuade them.
I have to do that.	I can choose the right response.

I have used this chapter to explore the concept of institutionalization, allowing you the opportunity to assess whether you consider yourself to be institutionalized or not. If you do feel you are institutionalized, and you want to take back control of your own destiny and promote your independence, then the next chapter will explain how this can be achieved.

R U listenin'?

- We are all susceptible to institutionalization.

- Some people make a conscious decision to be institutionalized.

- Institutionalization can be seen as a release from responsibility.

- We can never be truly content if we are institutionalized.

- Institutionalization takes away your identity.

Chapter 9

Rehabilitation

 When a successful person is asked, 'Did you expect to be successful?' they will respond with the answer, 'Yes.' The magnitude of their success may be greater or less than they expected, but they do not see themselves as failures. This is often the difference between a person who is institutionalized and one who is not. A person who is institutionalized would not visualize a positive future for themselves because they do not believe they have any control over it. We may not be able to dictate our future but we are able to direct it.

Marco: Arson – three years

When I arrived on the wing, Marco was kicking the living daylights out of his cell door from the inside and it took me a while to calm him down. I used my favourite technique of speaking slowly and softly, which forces the listener to be quiet and concentrate if they want to hear you. Eventually he calmed down and promised the officers he would behave if they allowed him out of his cell to talk to me. My first and obvious question was to ask why he was giving his door GBH (Grievous Bodily Harm).

He wanted to go to the gym but had been refused because of his poor behaviour. I queried why he wanted to go and his answer was a casual 'Because I want to exercise.' I asked him specifically what exercise programme he wanted to do but he could not answer. I suggested he got a copy of the programmes available in the gym, study them and decide which programme would be most beneficial to him. Reluctantly he agreed.

I used the opportunity to analyse his behaviour. He believed that screaming and shouting was the only way to be heard whereas I, on the other hand, believed that as an adult he should not be screaming and shouting for anything. He had lost the ability to take control of his own behaviour and he relied on others to respond to his outbursts and take decisions for him. I believed that his behaviour was a direct result of being institutionalized and what he needed to do was to take control of the situation.

At our next meeting he had done as I suggested, and said he was keen to do the weightlifting programme because he would receive a certificate. Knowing I had him focused, I wanted him to be proactive and display his independence and so, together, we put his name down for the weight-lifting programme and we also went to the library to select a physical-fitness book. From this book of exercises he designed his own workout regime which he could follow in his cell while still focusing on the gym programme he had selected. Eventually his application for the gym programme came through and because his behaviour had been excellent he was allowed to start the programme. Even though Marco was locked in a cell, it had not prevented him from remaining in control of his life. He had taken responsibility for himself, identified a goal to aim for and taken control of his own destiny. He had disempowered those in authority, and he needed to continue in this frame of mind if he was to avoid becoming institutionalized.

Exercise 9: Rehabilitation

Group and individual exercise; see Chapter 15.

Karl: Robbery – four years

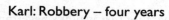

Karl was a man who loved nothing more than to question every piece of advice I offered him. You never had a conversation with Karl – it was always a debate. One day he attended a session I was delivering which focused on the four steps to independence we should consider when taking control of a situation.

1. Make a decision, not an excuse.
2. Have a strategy.
3. Take a risk, if required.
4. Learn from your successes/failures.

No sooner had I written the four independent steps on the white board than Karl informed me that I had written the four steps every criminal should obey when contemplating an earner (an illegal activity to make money). He went on to explain how he had obeyed the steps when committing his crime:

1. He had made a decision to rob from a garage.
2. He had a strategy because he had surveyed the garage and knew when the till would be full.
3. He took a risk. He entered the garage disguised in a mask with what appeared to be a weapon in a bag.
4. His four-year sentence had taught him not to remove his mask before leaving a garage with CCTV.

On the surface I could not disagree with Karl because he appeared to have considered the four independent steps. However, what he failed to appreciate was:

1. He had not taken a decision – he had made an excuse. He had no money and believed the only way for him to obtain money was to steal it.

2. He did not have a strategy. A strategy is a long-term plan and he was seeking instant gratification.

3. He did not take a risk because a risk implies the possibility of incurring misfortune or success. Karl's actions were destructive to all involved.

4. Karl had not learnt from the experience. He believed his four-year sentence had taught him not to remove his mask before leaving the scene of a crime. What he should have done was look at his life in the bigger picture and learnt that a life of crime was destroying his chances of a life of contentment.

Making a change

People I consider to be institutionalized have made the following statements:

- I let other people make the decisions because that way it's never my fault.

- I hate my job, but there are no other jobs available.

- I have always been unlucky.

- No one ever gives you a break in life.

- Life has a way of keeping you down.

- If only I had received a good education as a child.

If you believe you may be institutionalized, try identifying a statement you use that confirms your belief and write it down. As a guide, most statements made by people who are institutionalized start with 'If only,' 'I must,' 'I can't.' For example, 'If only I had received a good education as a child.'

Now, following the four independent steps, consider a change you wish to make in your life. Draw up the four steps and identify how you will take control and achieve your objective as shown in the sample below.

Remember, practice and commitment are key to your well-being. If there was an Olympic medal for excuses, people who are institutionalized would win it because they have the best excuses for not being proactive. If this is a trait in yourself then you might want to be made aware of it. Faced with a difficult

1. Make a decision, not an excuse
I will improve my education.
2. Have a strategy
I will investigate evening classes and distance-learning programmes.
3. Take a risk if required
I have identified a programme but it will cost me £300.
4. Learn from your success/failures
I enjoyed my programme and will sign up for the advanced programme next year, OR, I found the programme very difficult and so next year I will need to set aside more time for studying.

decision in your life, do you make an excuse or do you follow the four steps I have just outlined?

As always, words are free but actions show a belief in your ability to make a difference and you need to think of them as an investment. Today is always the best day to start an investment in your future contentment. Failure to address your concerns is a lost opportunity to recognize a life of contentment.

If you believe you are institutionalized and you are scared to do anything about it – fine. What you may be lacking is self-discipline or the ability to set your own objectives and achieve them. Self-discipline and time-management will be explored in the next chapter, Know your Jailers.

R U listenin'?

- Recognizing you are institutionalized is your first step to independence.

- Independence is your right, not a privilege.

- Independence will allow you to plan your future.

- Independent people are attractive to others.

Chapter 10

Know your Jailers

In the 1860s a group of medical and scientific specialists were brought together to form a board that was responsible for identifying appropriate punishments for convicted criminals. Their remit involved making mathematical calculations of given tasks that prisoners should perform. Mechanical devices were invented to administer the punishments including a treadwheel and a crank handle, both of which served no purpose. The prisoner was required to tread the mill for a given amount of steps per day and the crank handle was turned on the same principle. As the handle wore and the turning became easier, the person employed to monitor the prisoner tightened a screw to ensure the task remained difficult. The prisoners referred to this individual as the 'screw' (prison officer).

Could you be an officer?

The key to success in prison is 'discipline' and the officers are the people who are expected to enforce it. Their black-and-white uniforms, shiny buttons and shoes are there for a reason, namely to display an air of authority. They tread the fine line of delivering discipline both as a punishment and a reward. In order for the prison to function, the officers must ensure that the many rules are obeyed by both prisoners and staff and that all daily routines are adhered to. The rule most prisoners are aware of is the discipline rule 47. This rule explains all the acts considered punishable if committed by a prisoner:

- Assault.
- Detaining another person.
- Denying an officer access to part of the prison.
- Fighting.

- Intentionally endangering the health of others.

- Obstructing an officer.

- Escaping/absconding.

- Breaking the rules of temporary release.

- Possessing an unauthorized article.

- Selling an article to another prisoner.

- Selling one of his or her own possessions.

- Taking another prisoner's belongings.

- Setting fire to the prison.

- Destroying or damaging property.

- Not being in the right place at the right time.

- Being disrespectful to an officer or visitor.

- Using abusive, threatening or insulting words/behaviour.

- Refusing to work/work properly.

- Disobeying rules.

- Offending against GOAD (good order and discipline).

- Committing/inciting others to commit any of the 20 offences already set out.

This rule also sets out the punishment that can be inflicted on a prisoner who commits any of the above offences.

Any person wanting a career as a prison officer must be prepared to go through the rigorous training to qualify. They are trained in all the disciplines of the service and expected to obey given orders regarding their appearance and attitude. They must obey all prison procedures and will be reprimanded and possibly dismissed if they fail to maintain an acceptable standard of discipline. An observer viewing the training of an officer will note that trainers are slowly shifting the emphasis from discipline to self-discipline. Although initially the trainees follow instruction, they will ultimately be responsible for their own actions, and so it is important that everything is second nature to them by the end of their training. When this happens the individuals will have achieved the level of discipline required. The ability to follow orders requires self-discipline and those who fail to achieve the required level of self-discipline will be rejected by the service.

Officers come in all shapes and sizes. They are not, as many people imagine, all six foot six inches, and they do not spend the majority of their time either wrestling with prisoners or dressing up in riot gear. They are involved in the daily care and supervision of prisoners and their duties may include supervising family visits, prison workshops, manning the emergency control room, security searches and also working with specialists such as probation officers, doctors, psychologists and education staff. Some of the skills and qualities considered important to be a prison officer are:

- Empathy.

- Patience.

- Integrity.

- Confidence.

- Consistency.

- Fairness.

- Sense of humour.

- Physical fitness.

This list could be applied to any job that involves supporting other people. It is a 'wish list' of skills and qualities that any manager would want their staff to be able to display in their daily routine. A person with these skills and qualities should also possess a healthy self-esteem, but unfortunately this has not been my experience in the prisons I have worked in. I have met prison officers who were well-balanced and highly motivated to support those in their care but did not treat themselves with the same care.

How can you trust the person who ensures you stay in jail?

Why are we often able to project certain qualities that support others and yet not be able to support ourselves in the same way?

On numerous occasions I have met or read of prisoners who identified particular officers who, through their support, were able to change their lives. Why only some prisoners – why not all prisoners? It could be because not all officers have the necessary skills, or it could be because not all prisoners are prepared to accept the support of someone they see as their jailer.

When you are trapped in negative feelings about yourself, do you ever consider who your jailer is? Is it your boss at work, your partner, a family member, a friend, or is it yourself? If you are your own jailer, are you similar to the prisoner who feels unable to trust the advice of the officer who locks him in his cell every night? Are you unable to trust your own advice? In many cases people who go to prison are people who have not accepted the rules of society. If you do not discipline yourself then someone else will do it for you. We are all in the same boat. If you do not pay your bills or you act inappropriately at work, you will find your bank manager or boss disciplining you.

There are times in our daily life when we decide it would be nice to be fit and healthy and we may even make a telephone call to our local gymnasium to enquire about the price of membership. However, the telephone call may be as far as we go towards our new keep-fit regime, because we munch on some junk food while sipping alcohol and decide we do not have what it takes to motivate ourselves. Could this be a page from your diary?

No one is perfect. We all have our bad habits and excuses that we wish we could dispose of, such as smoking, drinking, eating too much, complaining about being tired and not having the time or energy to keep on top of the numerous jobs around the house. Self-discipline will offer you the key to tackle all the above.

Self-discipline gives us the stamina required to recognize our goals. It gives us the tools to deal with hardships and difficulties whether they are physical or emotional. It teaches us to seek the greater reward and reject the need for instant gratification. The more we develop our self-discipline the greater its strength becomes and the more pleasure we receive from our well-being.

The way in which we perceive the world around us and our ability to discipline our emotions, will affect the way we behave and react to given situations. If you believe self-discipline requires an enormous amount of effort and hard work, then you probably do not have it. Those who have self-discipline know that the rewards it offers far outweigh the commitment required. If people who do not have it put as much effort into developing their self-discipline as they do complaining about not having it, they would have self-discipline spilling out of their ears.

Self-discipline is a strength and the more you work at it the stronger it becomes. To strengthen your self-discipline start with simple goals and work your way up to the greater goals that you have always desired but never felt able to recognize. Remember, the idea of joining the gym is a big goal and so start with something more achievable, like polishing your shoes everyday.

Bruno: Assault – two years

Bruno worked as a doorman at a nightclub in London and one night he was involved in a scuffle outside the club. He punched a man until he was unconscious and the man remained in a coma for three months before making a slow recovery. I asked Bruno to write a piece of work about a time in his life when he felt in control.

I must have been about 13 years old – I will never forget the day. It was very sunny as I walked to my local boxing gym. I was always proud when I walked to the gym, and wanted to tell everyone where I was going. What I did not want them to ask me was if I had won any of my fights. The answer was no. Even though I had not won a fight I loved going to the gym and watching all the men working out and boxing. They treated me like an adult and encouraged me to train hard. There was a big sign on the wall that read, 'Self-discipline is not a punishment – it's a pleasure'. I had a fight that day and was feeling apprehensive. I had worked hard to be allowed to fight, but based on my previous fights I knew the towel would be thrown in if I so much as winced.

I spent the morning before the fight practising a combination of punches my coach had been teaching me. He kept telling me I was too slow and I need to work out with lightweights and concentrate on speed. Entering the ring I had my usual butterflies. One of the reasons why I believe I had lost fights before was not my ability, but my butterflies. Very little happened in the first round – that helped settle my nerves. I had tried to put together the combination of punches we had been working on, but they failed to have any impact. Then in the second round I delivered a textbook combination of punches to the side of the body, bringing my opponent's guard down. Finally an upper cut sent him crashing to the floor. The crowd cheered and I knew right there and then that I had what it took to be a boxer. I was in complete control of my mind, emotions and body. Everything I had ever wanted was granted to me that day. It was payback time for all the self-discipline I had shown training in the gym. Self-discipline had brought me rewards beyond my expectations and I wanted to have more experiences like this in my life.

Achieving contentment in our lives requires positive thoughts and behaviour and neither are obtained without self-discipline. Once we teach ourselves self-discipline we can apply it to all areas of our lives – anything from cleaning the car to controlling our emotions in difficult times.

We should first taste self-discipline as children

As children we are often introduced to discipline in a negative format. A child who has been unfairly disciplined might react by refusing to develop self-discipline because they associate it with punishment. Equally, a child who has been overindulged, or who has experienced undisciplined adults may not develop self-discipline either.

The children who lack self-discipline usually work on instant gratification. They are not prepared, or are not aware of the need to learn delayed gratification (being patient) until they achieve what they really want. If they do not learn delayed gratification they will be dissatisfied because they seek to fulfil their needs time and again with no actual recognizable outcome. Setting goals offers them the focal points they need.

Children can learn by adults talking to them about how they discipline themselves. Children who grow up with no self-discipline will become unhappy adults. If you feel that your self-discipline has been compromised in your development, you are not alone. It is, however, up to you to identify your concerns and correct them. You can instil the self-discipline you require to change yourself regardless of your past experiences and how you have behaved.

Steps to strengthen your self-discipline

1. Keep it simple. Start by addressing simple and quick jobs around the home.

2. Get focused. Concentrate on being tidy.

3. Be efficient. Get into the habit of putting things back where they belong and if they have no specific place, make one.

4. Break your routine. Instead of coming home from work and putting the television on, go straight to the kitchen and prepare a quality meal.

5. Sacrifice a pleasure. For a month, stop taking milk in your tea or coffee.

6. Monitor your vocabulary. For a month, try to avoid any negative feedback to yourself or a colleague. If you need to be negative try being diplomatic.

7. Stop wasting time. Avoid junk TV and magazine articles, and gossip at work.

8. Be the best. Decide to do all tasks to the best of your ability – anything from a minor task such as ironing a shirt to the bigger tasks you may be employed to do.

9. Monitor your behaviour. Recognize when you are feeling lazy and do something about it before it gets a grip on you.

Self-discipline is a big contributor to your self-esteem. It is the driving force behind your belief in yourself and your ability to achieve. Knowing you are in control of it will give you the peace of mind you require and the skills necessary to participate in all areas of your life.

Establishing your goals will be the benchmark you use to monitor your self-discipline and these goals will help you to draw up the disciplines you need to be successful. Your discipline will be rewarded constantly, not only when you achieve your goal, but each time you behave or think in a constructive way towards reaching your goal.

You should measure your progress. If you fall off track but manage to bring yourself back – well done. This is self-discipline at its best. Recognizing you have lost your way and correcting the error is what self-discipline is all about.

Time management

Time management is an integral part of the self-discipline equation. Often when people talk about self-discipline their sentences end with 'I wasted my time' or 'I wish I had the time again'. Time is a great tool in developing your self-discipline.

Time cannot be bought – it is a gift. How precious is it? Imagine you have been given one year to live. Make a list of all the things you would do, the people you would see, the places you would visit and the life you wish you had had. Bring yourself back to the present, appreciate you are not in this predicament and feel compassion for people who are not as fortunate as yourself. Start showing time the respect it deserves. Remember it's a gift, do not waste it. It is important to structure our lives to ensure we are making the most of our time and learn to stop stressing about matters within our control. Drawing up a time-management plan allows us to free up our mind.

Exercise 10: Know your jailers

Group exercise; see Chapter 15.

If you are still struggling with your discipline, consider physical fitness as it is a wonderful way of learning self-discipline. Physical exercise has obvious rewards, however, one of the main benefits and a reason why people get addicted to it is the release of endorphins from the brain. Endorphins are the body's natural 'happy' drug and because they are morphine-based, they give us that 'feel good' factor. The next chapter will explore endorphins and the many other benefits of physical exercise.

R U listenin'?

- Squander time at your own expense.

- Self-discipline is a pleasure – not a punishment.

- If you do not discipline yourself – someone else will do it for you.

- Introduce self-discipline into your life – do not demand it overnight.

- Self-discipline will give you control over your own life.

Chapter 11

The Gym

 I worked with a young man named Scott who produced some stunning artwork, which was mainly portraits, but he also did some surreal work. When he was released from prison he wanted to set himself up in business as a free-lance artist and so I tried to arrange a grant from a charity to enable him to buy the equipment that he required. As a reward for his dedication, the governor had granted him permission to leave the prison for the day to enable him to visit the Koestler Exhibition. The Koestler Awards are held once a year and are given for pieces of creative work produced by prisoners. I had agreed to accompany Scott to the Koestler Exhibition in London.

On the day, I expected Scott to be excited about the exhibition but this did not appear to be the case. I was disappointed in his lack of enthusiasm and began to believe I was wasting my time. We had to travel by train from the Midlands to London and once we had arrived in London and began using the Underground he started dragging his heels and made no effort to keep up with me. I practically had to hold on to him when jumping on and off the trains to ensure I did not lose him. Expecting him to climb stairs at the tube station was like asking him to make an Everest expedition. Walking through the busy London streets I wished I had never bothered taking him to the exhibition. I began to wonder if his intention was to go AWOL (absent without leave). Was he biding his time and waiting for the right moment? That, of course, was his choice. I had no intention of trying to prevent him – I would report the incident, have a pub lunch and go to the exhibition on my own.

In the end I became tired of his behaviour and eventually confronted him about it. I questioned whether his interest in attending the exhibition was genuine. He informed me that he was excited about the exhibition, but it was his lack of physical fitness that was his problem.

Scott attributed his lack of physical fitness to living in a six-metre cell for 12 months with an en-suite toilet, showers at the end of the corridor, and having all his washing and food delivered to his wing. The only real exercise he got was at the gym and because he found it boring it was difficult to motivate himself. He had read the magazines that tell you to get off the bus a stop early to take in more exercise and to climb the stairs instead of taking the lift. He told me 'In prisons there are no buses, no lifts and if you try and walk fast the screws think you are up to no good and tell you to slow down.' My naivety had got the better of me. Scott actually was the genuine young man I believed him to be but it was his physical fitness or lack of it that made him appear lethargic. A prison may sound like a hotel, with someone else to do all your fetching and carrying, but in reality it is not by choice that prisoners do very little. The strict regime they must obey prevents them from doing a great deal. There are no luxuries about being imprisoned: it's boring and repetitive – and tipping is optional! It is a breeding ground for institutionalization.

Prison exercise

Prisoners, on the whole, are committed to attending the gym and this is quite understandable when a trip to the gym may be the highlight of their day. In my experience not many prisoners maintain their enthusiasm for the gym when they are released.

Prisons recognize the importance of physical fitness and the majority are well-equipped. They have weights and fitness rooms, sports halls, astroturf and grass pitches. I have even worked at one prison where they had a climbing wall, although teaching prisoners to scale walls is something that has always amused me. The qualifications that are on offer vary from prison to prison but they can include personal awards for weightlifting, leadership, first aid and also job-related awards for those wishing to work in the fitness industry when they are released. The role of the staff is to use the gym not only to educate prisoners in physical fitness, but also to encourage mental fitness.

The main focus of the physical education department's criteria is to develop the individual's physical fitness but also to help prevent further offending. Physical education programmes are designed to tackle criminal behaviour through achievement and a sense of well-being.

Prison Service physical education objectives:

- Self-awareness – an understanding of our thoughts and feelings.

- Self-esteem – the beliefs we hold about ourselves that could affect our ability to achieve.

- Controlling aggression – understanding the role agression plays in our lives.

- Exploring and managing feelings – understanding our feelings and how to control them.

- Communication – how we relate to others and ourselves.

- Negotiation – agreeing outcomes to satisfy all concerned.

- Reviewing skills – the ability to reflect upon personal behaviour.

- Interpersonal skills – the skills we demonstrate when addressing all the above.

Looking after your body regularly can develop all of the above but I am not convinced that prisoners and people in general appreciate the impact physical exercise can have on our mental well-being. In this chapter I want to explore the reasons why we should take regular exercise as a way of exercising our minds as well as our bodies. I cannot emphasize enough the importance of the effect physical exercise will have on your well-being, but I will try.

Health through exercise is often measured by the following methods:

1. A decrease in blood pressure. (Blood pressure is the pressure of the circulating blood against the walls of the arteries, the veins and the chambers of the heart.)

2. Improvements in lipid profile. (Lipid profiles are tests that indicate whether someone is likely to have a heart attack or stroke caused by blockages of blood vessels.)

3. Increase in bone density (strengthens the bone against injury, i.e. a fracture.)

4. A decrease in body fat. (Fat is an excellent source of energy which is fine as long as that energy is being used up.)

5. Improvements in overall well-being (healthy self-esteem.)

All are said to have an impact on our cardiovascular (heart's) health.

The reason why I cannot detail the perfect exercise routine is because I am not a qualified fitness instructor. We all have different physiques and so, therefore, people require different amounts and types of exercise. The majority of health centres recommend 60 minutes of exercise three times a week and that your heart should be working at 50 to 70 per cent of your maximum heart rate for your age. What I can do, however, is eliminate the age-old excuses about not having enough time to exercise. Exercise literally gives you time, because you will live longer.

From an early age we all know the importance of exercising in order to maintain a healthy body. However, what is not emphasized is the effect on our well-being. Exercise has a direct effect both on the way we feel about ourselves and our ability to cope with daily stresses and strains.

Exercise 11: The gym

Group exercise; see Chapter 15.

Roger: Conspiracy to defraud – five years

Roger was referred to me after staff noticed he appeared low. This seemed odd because he only had a few months of his sentence left and everyone expected him to be happy. My first opinion when meeting him in the gym was that he defied my understanding of the benefits of exercise. He was a powerful-looking man whose physique was that of a man who regularly visited the gym and followed a balanced diet. To my way of thinking he should have been a well-balanced individual. However, whenever we spoke he appeared negative and frustrated.

I decided to watch him working out and I found that his regime was beyond anything I would recommend. He was fanatical. My first note of concern was his decision not to have someone spot him (spotting is to have a buddy who is ready to help you with the weights if you are struggling) and then I noticed the look on his face before lifting the weights. He looked at the weights as though they had just told him he had an extra six months added to his sentence. On completion of his workout I tried to talk to him but I was met with a wall of silence.

I realized he was lifting his weights by placing himself in a state of raging anger. He did not want anybody's support or advice. He was alone and on a mission to prove a point. He attended the gym to take revenge on all the times in his life when things and people had let him down. Every time he lifted a weight he was proving a point to someone, somewhere in his life. This offered him the motivation to lift the weights but ultimately it was promoting his negative attitude to his life in general.

My objective was to make Roger enjoy exercising. I did not want to discourage his training but I did want to discourage the anger he generated in order to complete his training. I wanted to introduce other forms of exercise and, in particular, a team sport where he would be forced to liaise with others to achieve. In short, I wanted him to have fun.

I put my observations to Roger in a very mild way (as one does when nego-tiating with a person whose biceps looked bigger than my waist) and he was quite amenable. This could have been because he thought it would look good in his parole report (the report that will look at a prisoner's discretionary early release under supervision) or maybe he was just waiting for someone to tell him what he already knew. I suggested he tried a few of the sports on offer at the prison and to my surprise he agreed. We soon discovered he had two left feet and little coordination and so it was no surprise that he failed to enjoy any ball sports. I was running out of ideas when I suddenly thought about badmin-ton. However, he was reluctant to try it as he saw it as a feminine game and not in keeping with his macho image.

He did however, give it a try, and found that he could display power and technique without aggression and brute force. He never really mastered the game – I believe the game mastered him – but he became more sociable and occasionally even laughed. He cut back on his weight training and began to coach some of the younger prisoners with their weight training. He learnt to enjoy exercise and not see it as a way of expressing his anger. I believe the social impact I was hoping team sports would have upon him took place, because he became far more relaxed and began enjoying his exercise rather than seeing it as a challenge.

Biological effects of exercise

Scientists believe that exercising releases endorphins which produce a natural high and gives the individual a feeling of healthy well-being. Your endorphins are your body's 'happy drug'. Endorphins are substances which are chemically related to morphine and other opiates and act by blocking pain receptors in the brain. Exercise is a way of releasing the endorphins and result in making you happy for a few minutes or hours. Some people believe they are addicted to exercise but in actual fact they are more likely to be addicted to the release of endorphins.

Dangerous activities also release endorphins, hence the reason why some people are drawn to dangerous sports such as car racing, skydiving and bungee jumping. Criminals may experience endorphin rushes when they are being chased by the police or breaking into a bank. You do not have to risk your life to enjoy endorphins. Activities like meditation, deep breathing, laughter and sex are other ways of releasing endorphins.

Endorphins are good for your health because they help to:

- reduce stress

- relieve pain

- postpone the ageing process

- boost the immune system against diseases and killer cells.

Our immune system is not only in place to fight off nasty bacteria, but it will also benefit from regular exercise and support our well-being. Factors such as stress have the potential to lower our immune system, which can leave us wide open to attacks on both our physical and mental well-being. The figures for people attending doctors' surgeries for stress-related illness are greater than any other diagnosis. Stress attacks the body's resources and results in the lowering of coping functions making us feel run down and open to illness.

Prevention is the best cure. It is better to take regular exercise now rather than wait for the onset of negative beliefs and emotions, which make it difficult to motivate ourselves. It you're not already exercising then you should start because negative emotions suppress immune functions. Positive attitudes and the ability to indulge in humour have a direct impact on our immune system and promote our self-esteem.

Do you know what type of exercise you prefer?

Identifying the right type of exercise for you is crucial to your well-being. Are you the type of person who enjoys a high intensity workout and who needs to be dripping with sweat before they feel they have had a proper workout? Or are you more of a social animal who prefers a team sport, which involves a chat and a drink after each session? Maybe you are the type of person who prefers to include some walking, swimming or cycling into their daily routine? In my experience a lot of people do not know what type of exercise they prefer, simply because they have not seriously tried different styles of exercise. Or, they may have gone along to a gym with a friend and had a really bad experience trying to lift weights, jumped around in an aerobics class, attempted a circuit training session or simply felt paranoid about the way they looked in a pair of shorts.

The environment you exercise in may affect your mood. Some people are happy to exercise in a gym, with the latest pop music blaring in the background whereas others prefer a run outdoors in the fresh air. Identifying the correct mode of exercise for you will determine whether you keep a balanced life that includes exercise.

If you have tried joining the local gym and then failed miserably on the treadmill or simply stopped going due to boredom, then join the queue. You need to try a variety of exercise regimes. Try the different classes on offer at your local gym until you find one that suits you or just keep rotating your classes. For example, you may want to try an aerobic exercise or a sport you have never done before. Think beyond the treadmill and the bench press. Sports centres and colleges are now catering for all ages and levels and know that keeping fit is a big moneymaker. However, keeping fit does not have to be prohibitively expensive, for example, running outdoors will cost you a pair of running shoes and a kagoole for the rainy weather. If you enjoy the social aspect of exercise then try joining a group of people whose company you enjoy. If you find yourself in a group of people you cannot relate to, look around and try another group. In theory, exercising should bring out the best in you and the people around you and this makes for a pleasant environment to be part of. The self-discipline discussed in the previous chapter should help with the motivation you need to help you exercise, but below are some additional tips:

- When starting to exercise, be realistic about the amount of exercise you can do comfortably.

- Identify a person you could exercise with.

- Record the amount of exercise you do or the time it takes. This will help you gauge how you are improving your fitness levels.

- Distraction can also help. Try listening to music when you exercise.

- Set a goal and decide on a reward when you achieve it.

- Book your exercise time in your diary – make it a date.

- Vary your routine.

- Visualize the overall benefits as you exercise.

- Remember, being able to exercise is a privilege not a burden.

- Daily exercise is a way of spending quality time with yourself or socializing with other like-minded people. It should not be seen as a punishment. Its benefits are tenfold, deterring conditions such as obesity, high blood pressure and poor cholesterol levels. Exercise helps you tackle lifestyle habits that may lead to heart attacks and strokes later in life.

The benefits you can expect from regular physical activity are that it:

- keeps weight under control
- boosts energy levels
- prevents and manages high blood pressure
- counteracts anxiety and depression
- improves sleep patterns
- controls stress
- increases enthusiasm and optimism
- releases tension
- improves blood cholesterol levels
- improves circulation throughout the body
- prevents bone loss
- increases muscle strength
- improves self-image.

Sleep

I felt the need to mention sleep in this chapter, as it is vital to the energy we need to exercise. We do not need any scientific study to tell us how bad we feel when we do not get a good night's rest. Ensuring we have a good night's sleep will improve the quality of our life.

A good night's sleep will:

- ensure you have the energy you need to exercise
- keep you feeling calm
- improve your relationships with others
- improve your concentration
- make you feel more positive
- even help you to lose weight.

When we sleep the human growth hormone is released and this hormone repairs and helps rebuild lean body mass and bone. Lack of sleep will affect the level of repair and may even make you age prematurely. The body's cells also show increased production and reduced breakdown of proteins during sleep. As proteins are the building blocks needed for cell growth and repair, a good night's sleep is essential for combating the damage caused by factors such as stress. Sleep also helps to restore our immune system and it is worthwhile noting that while we are sleeping we are burning fat, provided we do not eat later than 8 pm and get to bed by 10 pm. If we don't then eat breakfast until 7 am this ensures we have at least 11 hours fasting to ensure maximum fat-burning time.

Exercise plays a big part in promoting a healthy sleep pattern and following the advice offered in this chapter should promote a good night's sleep. A healthy sleep pattern is not exhaustion – you do not have to exercise so hard that you crawl to your bed. Here are some further ideas you may want to consider:

- Avoid caffeine, nicotine and alcohol four hours before going to bed.

- Relax before going to bed, have a hot bath or read a mild book.

- Release any concerns. Write them down on a piece of paper.

- Treat your bed with respect. Place quality sheets and pillows on it.

- Decorate your room in peaceful colours, not with posters.

- Keep your bedroom clear of clutter, half-drunk mugs of coffee and bits of toast.

- Keep to strict sleeping times.

As I mentioned early on in this chapter, I am not in a position to detail the exercise most appropriate to you. This advice is freely available from any sports centre or doctor's surgery. I would recommend speaking to an expert to gauge the level of exercise appropriate for you, because if you lunge straight into a regime that does not suit you then, apart from leaving you in pain, it could put you off the joys and benefits of exercise.

Exercise and diet will influence your quality of life. Monitoring the amount of exercise you take every week will help you lead a balanced life. Your exercise regime and your diet go hand-in-hand and when both are balanced you should be able to enjoy the benefits of a well-balanced lifestyle. In the next chapter I will concentrate on the benefits of a healthy diet. We will explore the age-old quote 'you are what you eat', or sadly, in some cases, you are what you take away.

R U listenin'?

- Exercising promotes a healthy body and mind.

- Exercise will offer you a sense of achievement.

- Your style of exercise and where you do it is most important for you.

- Exercise will make you feel energized.

- The medical profession promotes exercise as the best natural remedy to many conditions.

- In the majority of cases, exercise should always be an alternative to prescribed drugs.

Chapter 12

Kitchens

 Although there are many reasons why people would not like to find themselves serving a prison sentence, the majority of them would relate to their loss of freedom. For me, because I have experience of prisons, food would be an integral part of my fear. It is not that the food in prison is not to an acceptable standard – it is. I have eaten in many an officers' mess (prison officers' canteen), where the food is prepared by the same people who prepare the prisoners' food, and found the food palatable. I have not sat and eaten with prisoners as this could be viewed as stealing food and would not be allowed.

My fear would be the knowledge that I would not be able to make myself a nice, fresh baguette filled with chicken and salad or wake up in the morning to some marmalade on toast and fresh coffee. The thought of a set menu cooked en masse and lining up with my plastic cutlery and crockery to eat in a communal environment everyday would be enough to stop me committing a crime. I would much prefer to be in front of the TV watching some football and munching on my baguette. I would even admit to missing washing and drying my dishes and stacking them neatly in the kitchen cupboard when I had finished.

Prison kitchens

 Prison kitchens are probably one of the very few places where a prisoner can experience a real working environment. The working hours are long (5.30 am to 6.30 pm) and the work is continuous, as they have to feed hundreds of prisoners 7 days a week, 365 days a year. There is nothing seasonal about the work – every sitting is usually a full house all year round and yet, surprisingly, jobs in kitchens are very much sought after. I personally believe this is because working in the kitchen offers a prisoner the opportunity to complete a day's work and experience the reward that work offers – namely self-esteem. Also the opportunity to eat freshly prepared food has to be an incentive.

It takes a lot of preparation and discipline to run a kitchen. Paid civilian staff supervise prisoners who are employed to prepare the food. The majority of prisons I have worked in will prepare food and transport it on hot trolleys to the wings where prisoners will serve it. The transportation of the food in trolleys and the time delay from cooking it to its arrival at the intended destination is often to blame for the food not being as crisp and fresh as both the catering staff and prisoners would like.

On average, prisons serve meals at 8 am for breakfast, 11.30 am for lunch and 4 pm for the evening meal. Prisoners often comment that the time between the evening meal and breakfast is too long. In 2007 chefs were working to a daily budget of approximately £1.80 per person which is reasonable compared with many large establishments who cater en masse.

Regular meetings are arranged between catering staff and wing representatives to review menus, the quality of the food and to monitor the prisoners' complaints or praises. The catering staff are committed to providing a healthy diet and to ensuring that the food is wholesome, nutritious, well balanced, well prepared and served. They are expected to adhere to the following requirements when producing menus:

- Reduction of fat intake, especially saturated fats which are thought to raise cholesterol levels in the blood.

- Promotion of starchy, fibre-rich foods such as wholemeal bread, potatoes, pasta and rice, together with fruit and vegetables.

- The reduction of sugar intake.

- The avoidance of excessive salt.

The following are offered:

Meat	daily
Vegetables	daily
Poultry	twice weekly
Fresh fruit	daily
Fish	twice weekly

Prison food can help improve the health of prisoners who have not been eating a healthy diet 'on the out'. There are a variety of reasons why they may have not been eating healthily including drug addiction, lack of education about healthy eating or simply just not looking after themselves. It is common for people to put on weight and start taking an interest in education. They display a greater ability to retain information and focus more when they are in prison. On the inside many prisoners (by their own admission) recognize that diet plays a big part in their behaviour.

Today's menus also cater for special diets, including those required for medical and religious reasons, as well as catering for ethnic minorities and vegetarians.

The following is a menu choice.

Breakfast	Cereal
	Croissant and marmalade
	Sausage, tomatoes, bacon and toast
Lunch	Cold Meats
	Pizza slice
	Poached fish
	Stir-fry
	Sliced meat
	With beans or rice, vegetables, potatoes or chips
Dinner	Italian vegetable risotto
	Spaghetti bolognese
	Chicken salad
	Smoked herring fillets with lemon butter
	Beef and potato stew
	Chicken soup with dumplings
Desserts	Fruit crumble and custard
	Yoghurt or fruit

Exercise 12: Kitchens

Group and individual exercise; see Chapter 15.

Aylesbury Young Offenders

A study was carried out by the research charity Natural Justice led by Bernard Gesch who is a senior research scientist at Oxford University's Physiology Department. A group of prisoners were given a multi-vitamin, mineral and fatty-acid supplement while another group were given dummy pills. The study showed that violent incidents were reduced by more than one-third in the group taking the supplement. By simply changing their diets, violent behaviour was reduced by 35 per cent.

The power of food

Mention the word 'diet', and most people cringe. They feel that it's a nasty word used to encourage you to 'buy into' the many food and fashion brands on the market. Unfortunately, the word has been used and abused for many years and I guess it will continue to be so for many more to come. This is sad, as the word diet is a beautiful word meaning 'way of life' and comes from the Latin word 'day'.

In this chapter I want to concentrate on the power of food to control our well-being. I am not a dietician and will admit to not being the healthiest of eaters myself. I have, however, witnessed the dramatic effect healthy eating can have on individuals. For me, healthy eating is as important as physical exercise (as mentioned in the previous chapter) and, together, food and exercise will have a great impact on your well-being. This is why I believe that the two chapters in this book, which concentrate on physical exercise and food, are the most important. What I do not want to do is write about diet as in 'losing weight' and having a 'perfect' body.

We are all familiar with the saying 'you are what you eat' but do you truly understand the statement? Every year your body literally recreates itself because almost every cell in your body will have been renewed. What you eat is used to recreate your cells and so 'the new you' is based on your diet. So if you think about it, by disciplining yourself about what you eat, you are able to create the new you. Unfortunately, for some people the saying should be 'you are what you take away'. Recreating yourself with take-away food will probably guarantee that you suffer from stress, anxiety and a host of other conditions, until you are eventually taken away in a large wooden box!

A healthy diet is essential for a healthy body. To provide for all our needs food must contain the right mixture of carbohydrates, protein, fat, vitamins and fibre. These are just some of the main nutrients needed in order to keep your body balanced and healthy. These nutrients are taken into the body as we eat, and then absorbed through the intestines during digestion. Once you understand what your body needs it is usually quite easy to eat a healthy diet by eating food which contains the important nutrients.

Most food substances need to be broken down or digested so that they are in a form that can pass through the body and be used. Powerful enzymes break down the swallowed food into liquid, from which the digested nutrients are absorbed and carried into the bloodstream to the parts of the body where they are needed. This is one reason why it is a good idea not to slurp cups of tea or juice when eating a meal, because the enzymes need to be given a chance to do their job. Do not flush the food into your system with drinks – it needs to be digested. An important use for these nutrients is to provide energy to power the body, as well as providing the building materials for making new cells and repairing organs. A lack of some of these important nutrients, particularly in children who are growing fast, can cause some serious health problems. However, for people living in western countries too much food is a more likely problem and deficiencies are not common.

Many people see food as having the upper hand in their life and are unable to resist its temptation. What they do not appreciate is that knowledge will offer you the power to resist. By understanding food and its function in our lives we can take control of what we eat. However, it is important to remember that there is a social side to eating. I would not recommend you stop meeting for a coffee, having your Friday night take-away, taking a cream tea or watching a film while munching on your popcorn. Eating a balanced diet should not be a punishment; the key is everything in moderation.

'Two for the price of one' and 'all you can eat for a certain price' can be seen in restaurants and take-aways across the country. If you accept the negative effects that overindulging in food, particularly junk food, can have on your well-being, then why do it? The answer could be that eating can be a way of suppressing negative emotions such as stress, anxiety, boredom, anger, loneliness and sadness. The quick-fix foods that we accept as part of society are the same foods that may be triggering our negative feelings in the first instance. Therefore, we may find ourselves responding to negative feelings rather than hunger pangs.

Palatable foods that are sweet and fatty may have the ability to relieve some of our negative feelings, as they chemically counteract stress hormones. The danger is that once we have educated ourselves to respond to our feelings with starchy, sweet, salty and fatty foods, we will see a deterioration in our health as we gain weight and increase our cardiovascular risk. Variety is important. We all tend to eat certain foods on a regular basis unaware that these foods could be the very ones affecting our well-being. There is evidence that food can lead to the following:

- Anxiety.

- Panic attacks.

- Cravings or food addictions.

- Depression.

- Aggression.

- Impaired memory.

- Insomnia.

- Fatigue.

Charlie: verbally abusing a police officer – cautioned

Charlie had a fiery temper and he often 'sailed close to the wind'. Eventually he received a caution for verbally abusing a police officer. People often ask me what the difference is between a caution and a conviction. A caution is a warning, but a conviction could mean that you have received a prison or community sentence. Charlie attended a course run by the probation office which dealt with anger, and during a conversation with a probation officer it was recommended that he consider a life in the forces. The officer had a profound impact on Charlie's outlook on life and he started thinking more long-term instead of just in the here and now. He began to look at his future and what it had in store for him. He realized he had nothing and so he took the advice of the probation officer and joined the army. In the army he trained as a chef and learnt to appreciate the effects healthy eating had on his own mood swings.

I met Charlie when he was working as a chef in a prison where I worked. His belief in a balanced diet for controlling the behaviour of prisoners was admirable and on more than one occasion he proved his theory by employing prisoners in the kitchen on the understanding that they would have to follow his strictly balanced diet. Staff and prisoners alike respected Charlie. As the kitchen jobs are some of the best in a prison, he was never short of new recruits.

I began to recommend to those prisoners that I felt genuinely needed help with their well-being to apply for jobs in the kitchen. Charlie would insist that they ate a balanced diet before employing them and, in the majority of cases, the changes were apparent for all to see. Some took a matter of weeks while others took months, but there was no denying the impact a balanced diet had on their behaviour.

 ## Balanced diet

Supermarkets are making it easier to follow a balanced diet by highlighting the GDAs (Guideline Daily Amounts) on their products. Similar GDA tables to the one below can be found on the packets of many products identifying calories, sugar, fat, saturates and salt per serving. I stress, however, that this is per serving and not the contents of the whole product!

Example:

A tin of beans from a supermarket may have the following information. The top line is the consumption per portion and the bottom is the percentage of the recommended daily intake percentage in a portion.

Example portion table

Calories	Sugar	Fat	Saturates	Salt
125 kcal	10.9g	1.1g	0.2g	1.3g
6%	12%	2%	1%	21%

It is important that you learn the daily intake of all five areas because this allows you to decide what products would offer you a balanced meal at a glance.

Below is your daily recommended intake suggested by supermarkets working on a daily intake of approximately 2100 calories. The majority of health authorities recommend women taking 2000 calories a day and men 2500. I would suggest following the supermarket recommendations but would also suggest you add a bit of common sense into the equation and see how you feel.

Supermarkets' average recommended daily intake

Calories	Sugar	Fat	Saturates	Salt
2100 kcal	90g	70g	20g	6g

By keeping to regular mealtimes and including the following foods as recommended by the Food Standards Agency, one should be able to maintain a healthy well-being. The following suggestions may not be the most interesting read in this book but I cannot emphasize enough the impact a healthy well-balanced diet will have on your well-being – it is absolutely vital.

Fruit and vegetables

Fresh, frozen or canned; 100 per cent juices and dried fruits. Aim for at least five portions from this group each day.

A portion is:

- 3 heaped tablespoons of cooked vegetables
- 1 cereal bowl of mixed salad
- 1 piece of large fruit such as an apple or pear or 2 smaller fruits such as satsumas or plums
- 1 handful of fruits such as grapes or strawberries
- 1 tablespoon of raisins or 3 dried apricots
- 1 small glass of 100 per cent fruit or vegetable juice.

However much you eat beans, other pulse vegetables, dried fruits and fruit juices they only count once per day. Because they are considered a starchy food, potatoes don't count towards the '5 a Day' target.

Bread, cereals and potatoes

Rice, noodles, oats, breakfast cereals, chapattis, pasta, sweet potatoes, yams, beans, lentils, and dishes made from maize, millet and cornmeal also come into this group. Base your meals on these kinds of foods, which should make up about one-third of your diet. As they are a good source of B vitamins, choose wholegrain, wholemeal, brown or high-fibre varieties wherever possible. Generally, people eat less than they should from this food group, so make sure you eat lots! Try serving larger portions of these foods at mealtimes by, for example, having more rice or potatoes.

People often think that starchy foods are particularly fattening. This isn't true, but starchy foods can become fattening if they're either cooked or served with fat. For example, it's the margarine or butter we spread on bread, the cream or cheese sauce we add to pasta or the oil that we use for frying that makes them fattening. So cut down on these added fats rather than the starchy foods themselves.

Lean meat, poultry, fish and alternatives

For most people a healthy diet means eating only moderate amounts of meat, fish and alternatives such as lentils, nuts, beans and eggs and choosing lower-fat versions when you can.

Trim visible fat from meat, choose lean cuts wherever possible and remove skin from chicken before cooking. Meat such as bacon and salami and meat products such as sausages, beefburgers and pâté are all relatively high-fat choices, so try to keep these to a minimum. Beans such as canned baked beans and pulses are a good low-fat source of protein.

Aim to eat at least two portions of fish a week. This can be fresh, frozen or tinned. Each week, one of these portions should be oily fish such as sardines, salmon, pilchard, mackerel, herring, trout or fresh tuna (not canned tuna, although this is still a good source of protein and some vitamins).

Fatty and sugary foods

A healthy diet means eating and drinking less of these types of food. Eat foods containing fat sparingly and look out for the low-fat alternatives. This group includes margarine, butter, cooking oils and sugar, so it means fewer fried foods, crisps, biscuits, pastries, cakes and sugary drinks and less mayonnaise, cream, chocolate and other confectionery. Sugary foods and drinks should be limited as much as possible as they can quite often contribute to tooth decay.

Milk and dairy foods

Milk, cheese, yoghurt and fromage frais. For a healthy diet most people should eat moderate amounts of these foods. Low-fat versions are better for general healthy eating and also if you're trying to lose weight. Try semi-skimmed or skimmed milk, low-fat yogurt (0.1 % fat or less), virtually fat-free fromage frais and reduced-fat cheeses.

If you are not a great eater there are a variety of nutritional supplements on the market. However, I would stress the need to consult with a general practitioner before you start investing in various pills and potions. You should be able to make an appointment with your dietician through your local general practitioner or hospital. If you are on any medication they will be able to assess if changing your diet could impact on your well-being.

The most important liquid for a healthy body and mind is water. It acts as a transporter for nutrients such as vitamins, minerals and carbohydrates, while flushing the system out. The body is made up of two-thirds water. You should drink six to eight glasses a day and failure to do so will leave you feeling lethargic. You could consider drinking it when you have hunger pangs. Often it is your body's way of telling you that it is dehydrated. We lose as much as one-and-a-half litres of water per day through the skin and urine. The body could be calling out for water when really you believe it needs another sandwich or a chocolate bar. The secret is to keep one step ahead of your hunger, and taking in your daily quota of water will reduce your hunger. In other words do not wait until you are hungry to drink your water.

If you change your diet overnight even to a healthy one, the effect on your body can make you feel a lot worse rather than better. Introduce the changes in your diet gradually and this will also help you to monitor how you feel. You should be able to pinpoint the specific food that makes you feel better. Make the whole process more enjoyable by trying out new shops, foods and recipes. Expect some short-term side effects. Headaches and nausea are not necessarily indicators that certain foods disagree with you – they could be a reaction from your body as you reduce the food that you have become addicted to. If the symptoms persist, change your diet. These effects should also be evidence of the power that food has over your body and mind.

You must respect your own body if you are to be at peace with yourself. Monitoring what you put into your body will also give you a sense of control and discipline. Self-discipline is important for a life of contentment. Controlling our diet offers us the chance to impose self-discipline and the benefits far outweigh the consequences of any pleasures abusing our bodies may offer.

Here is a quick recap of what you should eat and why:

- Fibre: Keeps you regular.

- Protein: Important for growth and healing the body.

- Salt: Beware, too much will give you high blood pressure, possible stomach cancer and can lead to kidney failure, but you do need some.

- Vitamins: Help cells reproduce normally.

- Minerals: We require a variety of minerals. They supplement the body in numerous ways including the blood, bones, teeth, and cells.

- Carbohydrates: Give us energy.

- Fats: Are a good source of energy. They help us to absorb some vitamins and contain important things called essential fatty acids.

To all intents and purposes each chapter in this book so far has stood alone but we now need to look at the common denominator that pulls all the chapters together. There is one missing ingredient that will ensure we lead a contented life and enjoy a healthy well-being. In the next chapter we will explore the joys of maturity.

R U listenin'?

- Do not eat with your eyes and nose, in other words eat when you are hungry not when you are tempted.

- Appreciate the powers of dehydration; drink 6–8 glasses of water a day.

- Read food labels so that you know what you are eating.

- Taking control of your diet will help you take control of your well-being. You only get the one body, show it some respect.

Chapter 13

Freedom

Two questions I am regularly asked are, 'Why do people commit crime?' and 'How can we stop them?' For a long time it has been recognized that the reasons why many people get involved in crime can be as a result of a disruptive childhood, a lack of positive role models, lack of love or coming from a family of criminals. How can we stop them without having to lock them up? The answer is that 'we' cannot – they need to be stopping themselves. I have seen offenders offered numerous opportunities to change their lives and not taken them, while others have been offered just one chance and have grabbed it with both hands. So when does a person decided they have had enough of prison food? The answer is when they are ready to mature.

The prisoners I have worked with have given the following reasons for deciding to stop leading a life of crime:

- Personal relationships.

- Family responsibilities.

- Love.

- Influence of another person.

- Discovery of a hidden talent.

- Religion.

- Remorse.

- Family support.

Many people who are trying to sort out their own lives may use some or all of these reasons but, for me, each of these reasons has the potential to trigger the need for maturity. In this chapter I explore the ingredient, which links all the previous chapters together, namely the ingredient that ensures we are not prisoners of our own negative thoughts – maturity.

So what is maturity?

A bottle of wine matures 'physically' with very little effort – it just sits and waits. However, the rate at which we humans physically mature depends on our lifestyle and how well we do, or do not, look after ourselves. The major difference between humans and a bottle of wine (apart from the obvious ones) is the fact that we mature psychologically as well as physically. Our physical growth is visible for all to see but mental and emotional growth is not so predictable and also requires a lot more nurturing. The length of development is indefinite and the stages of development vary in individuals. Maturity is not guaranteed to come with age, but how we perceive and process given situations will help us to develop as individuals. Taking decisions based on facts, taking responsibility, challenging our own beliefs and differentiating (when required) between reason and emotion will help us to assess a situation without bias. We are then in a position to choose the most appropriate response for a given situation.

We all make mistakes, but how we react to difficult or stressful situations can often be a measure of our maturity and part of our maturity is being aware of our emotions and knowing when to express them. Our experiences as a child are vital to our development but in order to mature we must build on our experiences and emotions.

To identify maturity in an individual we may consider their age, their ability to make decisions, their intelligence and awareness of where they are at in their lives. To check if you are mature you may wish to consider the following.

- Are you open to new environments, knowledge and advice?

- Are you aware of your own responsibility for self-preservation?

- Are you philosophical and open-minded about new ideas?

- Are you in control of your emotions and can you make decisions based on your emotions or reason, as appropriate?

- Are you able to distinguish between assertiveness and aggression?

- Are you able to analyse your own beliefs, prejudices, assumptions and behaviour in an objective way?

- Are you able to appreciate the here and now?

- Are you honest with yourself and others?
- Are you able to strive for what you want from life without fear of failure or rejection?
- Do you take decisions based on facts?

Exercise 13: Freedom

Group exercise; see Chapter 15.

Leaving prison

Prisoners who have served their sentences are usually released from prison before 8.45 am and I often meet the early risers (prisoners released after breakfast) as I walk from the car park to the prison. For me, it is a strange experience because it's as if they are entering my world. I often visit their world behind the tall fences and barred gates but never expect them to enter my world. My world is a world of peace while their world is often one of turmoil and I do not want other people bringing their turmoil into my world. Then I realize that it's not my world – it's *our* world and to be more specific it's our lives. I ponder the question as to why I choose to work with people who have the potential to bring turmoil into my life. The answer is simple. I enjoy offering others my advice and guidance in the hope that they will learn the necessary skills to lead a life of contentment and peace and a life free of victims.

People react in different ways when they are released from prison. Some punch the air with a big smile on their face, others walk away as though they have just been scolded, while some look concerned by the 'what now scenario'. Faced with the pressures and temptations of the outside world, keeping out of prison becomes a challenge. Occasionally I am thanked by those released for the support I have offered, however, what really pleases me is when a person tells me they have not forgotten the advice I have offered and that they will put it into practice.

Walking into a prison one morning I met a man whom I had helped get on a training course when he was released. He joked about the threads (clothes) the prison had provided for him. The clothes he had come to prison in four years ago were too small and, in his words, 'out of fashion' and he then commented that they were like the clothes I was wearing that day. We spoke about the training course he would be attending and the positive response he had received from the employers he had written to. As we finished our conversation and exchanged pleasantries he made that classic quote, 'All I need in life is for someone to give me a break.' In my experience, getting a break that changes a person's life forever is rare and usually only ever happens in movies. There is no point in waiting for someone else to give us a break in life. If we accept that this is not going to happen then we have a greater chance of controlling our own destiny. The only person who gives us a break is ourselves and that break often comes when we are mature enough to accept what we can and cannot change in our lives. If we accept that remorse is the act of recognizing the error of our ways and making amends to correct them, then I believe we can experience a form of remorse when we address the negative beliefs we may have held on to for a large part of our lives.

Courts will always look favourably on people who show remorse. Once people have accepted responsibility for their actions the courts believe they are then able to confront the barriers their previous lifestyle has conditioned them to follow. Instead of looking for excuses to commit crimes, they are ready to address their concerns and work through them. By accepting they have behaved in such a manner that contradicts their moral code, they are displaying a level of maturity.

Peter: Commercial burglary – three years

I met Peter one day and he asked me to help him compile a business plan. He had about four months left of his sentence and was determined to change his ways. I had no idea how to write a business plan but Peter's enthusiasm and the fact that he seemed to have a good business idea (servicing caravans out of season), encouraged me to visit my bank manager for advice. Together, Peter and I compiled a business plan for his company and we approached various banks and organizations for support in his venture. Unfortunately we had no joy and so the idea got no further than the drawing board. Most people would have been disheartened, but not Peter – he never lost his enthusiasm, which I found intriguing.

Peter was a short, skinny man with protruding ears and this combination, together with the surname Pratt, made him the butt of many a joke. He had grown up in a household where his mother and father tolerated each other for the sake of their six children. Peter drifted through life aware of his mother's love for him and his father's neglect. He blamed his father's neglect for the life he now led. As a child, with no role model and no real friends, he began stealing from local shops to impress his peer group. He then advanced to motorcars and eventually he burgled industrial units.

Peter may have been disadvantaged in some ways but his greatest asset was his common sense and his ability to think through problems. I had a lot of time for Peter who showed genuine remorse for his behaviour. Over time he explained that his father had died while he was in custody and this had a profound effect on him. As Peter said, 'I woke up one morning and realized my time had come – I was now head of the family and responsible for my mother and five siblings.' In my opinion Peter had matured. He had stopped blaming others for the failings in his life and started taking control of his own destiny.

When Peter left prison he got a job in a garden centre and never returned to prison. Ten years later while driving in my car, a gardening truck pulled up next to me and on the side of it was an advert, which showed a picture of Peter with exaggerated facial features and looking very funny. Under it read 'Why work in the garden when you can get this Pratt do it for you'. Peter had worked hard, saved his pennies and opened a small garden centre. I was delighted at his success and admired the way in which he had turned around what others may have viewed as disadvantages into an advantage. He enjoyed the benefits of taking responsibility for his actions. Maturity had been good for Peter.

Monitor your maturity

We are all naughty children at some point because it's fun. We shed our responsibilities and expect others to monitor our behaviour and take the burden of responsibility off our shoulders. If we continue this behaviour into our adult life we run the risk of not maturing and when suddenly confronted with responsibility we struggle under the pressure. Our guardians often influence beliefs we develop in our childhood but this does not mean that they are always correct. They will dictate our thinking and behaviour, but as our surroundings and social situations change, failure to adjust our beliefs will inhibit the maturation process. Applying beliefs that were created when you were younger and functioning with different values, and then trying to make them 'fit' into your current situation may result in you experiencing negative feelings.

It is important to enjoy the moment as it happens. Concentrate on what you are doing and ensure that you are doing any given task to the best of your ability. Are you in touch with what you can realistically achieve? Are you able to differentiate between dreams and goals? Do you:

- display aggression when challenged about your beliefs?

- perceive a challenge as a direct attack on your very being?

- justify your beliefs with flimsy, or with little or no evidence?

- have negative feelings about yourself?

If we ask questions with the answer in mind then we will only hear the answers we want to hear. However, asking questions with no answer in mind equips us with the opportunity to develop our maturity. Learning must always be a pleasant experience and not a passive necessity. An inquisitive mind is a healthy mind. Questioning the validity of knowledge is crucial if we are to accept it as knowledge we can learn from; and if we use the same process to question our own irrational thoughts and behaviour we can develop our maturity. One of the signs of maturity is the ability to control our emotions. This can be observed by watching how people react to simple mishaps. It is important not to try to suppress emotions because to do so would create an imbalance in our lives. Emotions demand respect and discipline.

Although every moment in our lives is separate, cumulatively they will all impact on our future decision-making. Our behaviour now will be inherited by our future and we have a duty to invest in our future well-being now. Decisions made today should be made on an intelligent and rational basis and you should never criticize yourself for making an honest decision, regardless of the outcome.

These are some of the qualities of a mature person:

- They work with facts.

- They are not afraid of spontaneity.

- They place more emphasis on reason than emotions.

- They remain open-minded about all aspects of life.

- They think before they act.

- They are aware of the present.

- They take decisions based on knowledge not beliefs.

- They work to their limitations.

- They remain flexible.

- They acknowledge anxieties.

- They have a healthy self-esteem.

- They have a practical way of viewing situations.

Tony: Held at Her Majesty's pleasure

I was working as a supply trainer in a young offenders' institute and I had a class of about 12 who were reasonably well-behaved. I was delivering one of my personal development programmes about maturity when suddenly an alarm sounded in another classroom. There are usually two reasons why an alarm button is pressed – either a trainee is being silly and has pressed the button or a teacher has taken the decision that a situation is out of hand and the assistance of officers is required.

The trainees (young offenders are referred to as trainees) in my class jumped up from their seats and rushed to the classroom window to watch the officers running along the corridor to the classroom in question. With a bit of luck the individuals being removed from the classroom might not go willingly and there could be some action to watch. I sat in my seat and calmly asked the trainees to sit down and, while half of them did, the other half remained at the window. I was not in a disciplinarian mood that day and was, in all honesty, glad it was someone else's class and not mine kicking off (causing trouble).

The trainees eventually got tired of standing at the window and sat down. I played the situation down saying it must have been a false alarm but I also knew that it was unusual not to see a trainee being taken back to their cell by an officer. As I continued with my lesson I noticed more officers making their way to the classroom and eventually the classroom door opened and an officer informed me that all trainees were to return to their cells. As a supply trainer I was not too upset because I knew I would still receive my morning's payment even though I had only delivered an hour's work. I made my way to the staff tearoom to hear the gossip and find out what had occurred. An incident had taken place in one of the workshops where trainees were learning painting and decorating skills. A trainee aged 17 had used a sharp tool to stab another trainee aged 16.

The following day I entered the staff tearoom and was informed of the death of the trainee who had been attacked. I did not know either trainee but I still felt sad and confused about the sheer waste of two lives – the young man who died and his attacker who would now face a long prison sentence.

The following week I was asked to work with a young man called Tony in his cell because he was not permitted to mix with the rest of the prison popula-tion. It did not take me long to work out who the young man was. I went along to the segregation wing and explained to the officers who I had come to see. I was taken to Tony's cell and we sat on his bed and discussed his academic inter-ests. Why? He needed to be engaged because leaving him to sit in a cell 24 hours a day, 7 days a week would only add to his anxiety and make life difficult for everyone. We discussed his interests and agreed to practise some maths, English and art. I continued to see him a couple of times a week and while his maths and English were very basic, he did enjoy colouring in pictures. I supplied him with pastels, as I believed he could not harm himself or staff with them. Talking to him I realized he had lived his whole life avoiding any responsibilities that had the potential to develop his maturity. He was comfortable with the thought of a long prison sentence because his future was now mapped out; for the foreseeable future he would be cared for and could relax. There was no need to worry about finding employment, accommodation or wonder where his next meal was coming from because all his needs would be taken care of by Her Majesty. It would be a long time before he would be 'gate happy' (when a prisoner starts getting excited as they get close to their release date).

Exploring Tony's beliefs

I do not believe as a young boy Tony made a conscious decision to avoid the development of maturity – it just failed to evolve due to his hectic lifestyle. I do, however, believe he took a conscious decision to reject it later on in his life when he realized the responsibilities that accompanied it.

The following is an attempt to briefly explore each chapter from a maturity perspective and illustrate how Tony failed to respond in a mature manner.

Chapter 1: Prison Life

He lived his life in the present and had no long-term objectives. When he was not physically in a prison environment he was mentally. He had convinced himself that his life had no future and he was trapped in a mundane lifestyle where other people would take responsibility for his actions and punish him accordingly. I would accept that Tony's life to date had not been the best and even the fact that he had probably lived his life in response to his conditioning over the past 17 years, but what I could not accept was his belief that he could never recognize a life of contentment.

Chapter 2: An Accessory to the Crime

Tony's actions were destructive to himself and those around him. His behaviour guaranteed he had no friends and his family avoided him. At the age of 17 he had achieved nothing. He had become an accessory to the crime – the crime of an attack on his mental and physical well-being. He fitted the profile of an accessory to the crime by always talking himself down, never taking regular exercise, eating and drinking too much, getting angry with others, feeling lethargic, wallowing in self-pity, feeling lonely, not eating healthy food, worrying and wasting valuable time.

Chapter 3: Believing your Way Out from Within

His belief system was built on irrational beliefs about himself and the world that surrounded him. He failed to see the good in other people and was blinkered to the opportunities life offered.

Chapter 4: Knowing your Sentence

The environment Tony had grown up in had developed his belief system but what he failed, or refused to do, was recognize the inaccuracies of the beliefs he held and address them. He preferred to blame the world around him for his situation instead of learning insight into his own actions and addressing them.

Chapter 5: Natural Instincts

His daily needs were no different from other young men of his age but his problem was the way in which he recognized his needs. He spent a lot of his time running away from his needs and losing himself in drink and crime. Sadly, no one had managed to tap into his world and help him to explore why he felt the way he did. He refused to listen and built barriers to protect his belief system.

Chapter 6: Offending Behaviour

Like a lot of people in prisons, I guess no one had ever sat down and helped him to explore his needs. He was driven, as we all are, to satisfy his needs but it was the ways in which he addressed his needs that were inappropriate and destructive. Rather than being a productive member of society and benefiting himself and those around him, he lived a lifestyle that was more akin to the 'law of the jungle'.

Chapter 7: Segregation

Tony's actions segregated him both from himself and society. He was a prisoner in his own mind, surrounded by four walls which had been built from the following beliefs: that he should trust no one, it's every man for himself, attack is the best form of defence and look after number one. He failed to understand that the way we view and treat the world around us will be reflected in the way we treat and, more importantly, talk to ourselves.

Chapter 8: Institutionalization

He found comfort in the world of institutionalization. At an early age in his life he had never learned to take responsibility and was happy for others to lead his life for him. He would not actively get involved in the development of his well-being.

Chapter 9: Rehabilitation

While he was in prison he was encouraged to address his needs but given his state of mind, he failed to appreciate the joys of maturity and preferred to hold on to his irrational beliefs.

Chapter 10: Know your Jailers

Tony had never experienced discipline. Although he may have been beaten and battered by his father when he misbehaved, expelled from school, put into a secure unit (a secure detention home for young people) and then a young offenders' prison, he had not been disciplined. He had been institutionalized.

Chapter 11: The Gym

Tony never had a healthy release-valve – a way of letting off steam when he felt anxious or simply needed to burn off some calories. When he got anxious he looked for escapism through alcohol or a criminal activity. Chasing a football around a field or being part of a team that tasted success through a sport could have changed his life.

Chapter 12: Kitchens

Oblivious to the idea of a balanced diet, Tony ate poor-quality food. This made him a prime candidate for suffering from anxiety, panic attacks, cravings, food addictions, depression, aggression, poor memory retention, insomnia and fatigue.

Chapter 13: Freedom

Would Tony ever leave his own prison, the one he had created in his mind? Maturity is the key to all our development and it would also be the key to Tony's. Without developing maturity, Tony would serve his sentence (irrespective of the length of the sentence) and not recognize the need to take responsibility and grow as an individual. One day he would leave prison the same person he entered it, having learned nothing from his experience. If he decided to develop maturity while serving his sentence he would leave with a new set of beliefs and a greater understanding of himself. As I predicted, Tony was eventually sentenced to detention at Her Majesty's pleasure until he was considered safe for release.

Chapter 14: Sentence Planning

Tony would become familiar with the term 'sentence planning'. During his sentence, he would have regular reviews to monitor his sentence plan and ensure he was on target to complete it before ending his sentence. How much he would learn from his sentence plan was debatable.

Working with Tony was a period of reflection for me. In my line of work we are encouraged to reflect on our working practice – it's seen as part of our personal development, a type of self-audit. I tried putting into perspective the work I did with people and assess if it was of any benefit to them. It was possible that the only person who benefited from my advice and guidance was me, when I collected my salary.

I scanned the job papers and considered a career change but there were not many jobs advertised for a person who believed maturity is key to the development of individuals. The thought of a job where I sat behind a desk or a steering wheel did not appeal to me.

This was the only time in my career when I questioned the validity of my work. If I were a writer I would call it my 'dark period' but as I am not, I will call it my 'lock-down period' (lock-down in a prison is when everyone is locked up and no one is allowed to leave the prison – you have to sit and wait to receive permission to leave). An example of why this could happen is when a knife goes missing from the kitchen. A lock-down would be ordered by the governor and while the prison is searched, no movement is allowed around the prison by anyone. For me, it's a time when I sit and wait to be told when I can go home. Was I really having any influence on the people I advised or was I just ticking boxes? Were my words of wisdom having any effect on the people I advised?

It was around this time that I realized my strength was not in my ability to deliver a good training session on personal development (which I still pride myself on today) but my ability to listen and understand where people are coming from and want to go to. Listening forms a large part of my work, not just to the people I work with, but to myself. I practise what I preach. I develop my own maturity and am a better person for it.

Covering all the areas I have discussed in each chapter of this book, I sat down and reviewed my well-being. I was comfortable with my assessment of myself and I confirmed my belief in my ability to make a difference to people's lives. I stopped looking in the job papers and decided I was in the right job because through dealing with this young man I was able to remind myself of the joys of maturity and the need to 'keep listenin''.

In the next chapter, I will attempt to show you how, based on the prison service system of reward and punishment as well as the information I have offered throughout this book, we can learn to set and achieve our own objectives in a safe, constructive, achievable and enjoyable way.

R U listenin'?

- Maturity is a wonderful journey.

- Wisdom comes with maturity.

- Responsibility develops maturity.

- Maturity is a combination of logic and emotion.

- Without maturity we will not find contentment.

- We mature in all aspects of our lives.

Chapter 14

Sentence Planning

When I deliver a session on motivational techniques in prison, I start by asking the prisoners to tell me their release date. Everyone knows their release date off by heart. They will know their actual release date and also their early release date, which is granted for good behaviour. The objective of my exercise is to prove a point, which is that while they are in prison they have a goal in their lives – freedom – and the sooner they achieve it the better. The majority of prisoners are prepared to follow the disciplines of prison life in order to realize their goal. My concern, and a point I stress during my sessions, is the need to set goals before they are released from prison in order to motivate them when they leave. While many prisoners released do not set themselves goals, some do, and some set goals that are too ambitious to be achieved legally.

We all need goals, objectives, ambitions – whatever you wish to call them. We all need something to get us out of bed each day and motivate us to recognize our full potential.

The system used to structure the prisoner's time while serving their sentence and get them out of bed is called a 'sentence plan'. Sentence planning is designed to provide a positive structure of support and rehabilitation for the individual as they work towards their release date. If prisoners 'show willing' to achieve all the objectives set out in their sentence plan, they should receive early release.

The structure of the support offered while in custody is to identify skills the individual already has, tackle any behavioural problems and introduce them to new skills that could potentially make them more employable. Prisoners are offered the opportunity to progress within the prison system. This is the theory of sentencing planning but in my experience it is not always the practice, because places on training programmes, educational classes, support groups for drug addiction and cognitive therapy are limited. However, it is fair to say some of the people serving sentences will reject all the support offered, they will ignore their sentence plan and stagger through their sentence.

Sentence planning attempts to address the needs of people in custody and is based on common sense. The importance of sentence planning was highlighted in 1990 as a specific requirement after disturbances in prisons throughout the country. Governors realized that they needed to create a structured environment in which the prisoners were key players. Up to this point prisoners had been told what to do. After a few riots, it was realized that just maybe, they should have some say in their own future.

The prison service had recognized what the rest of the universe had known for a long time: that being part of a structured system with discipline can have a positive effect on the way we feel about ourselves and the environment we inhabit. If we respect the person or people in charge daily, we will not question their judgement and this allows us to work in an environment where we feel secure and do not fear our future prospects. Standardization is the key to continuity.

The importance of standardizing the sentence planning system and associated documentation was recognized and introduced. This provided a smoother transition and greater understanding of the objectives for the prisoners and staff. It meant that sentence plans could follow individuals to other institutions and allow them to maintain their level of achievement thus far. Ultimately a sentence plan can provide structure to an otherwise mundane lifestyle and offer a sense of purpose and goals to be achieved.

The disciplinary procedures used in a prison to run alongside a sentence plan are a system of levels. There are usually three, sometimes four levels within a prison which I have mentioned in previous chapters:

- Basic.
- Standard.
- Enhanced.

Would you benefit from a sentence plan?

A prisoner will wake up in the morning knowing what is expected of them in order to enhance their current level and meet the requirements of their sentence plan. Effectively they have a set of goals. You, on the other hand, will not have a sentence plan in place, which begs the questions:

- What are you aiming to achieve each day?
- What are your goals in life?
- If you have goals, what do you need to do to recognize them?
- How will you know when you have achieved them?
- What will you do if you do not recognize them?
- What support can you call on?

I believe we all need some form of sentence plan to structure our lives. We can all make New Year resolutions, but how many of us achieve them? More to the point, why do we not achieve them? Is it because we do not have a structured sentence plan? If you had a sentence plan what would be the difference between your sentence plan and that of someone in one of Her Majesty's prisons? The answer is that you will be your own disciplinarian, and you will be responsible for putting together the information about yourself required for your sentence plan. You will be the person in charge and the person you have to respect everyday. This in turn will strengthen your belief in your ability to achieve and you will not question your own judgement, which you may have been doing to date.

You may have realized by now what my next suggestion will be – design your own sentence plan. There is no need to call it a sentence plan as life is not a sentence but if you believe it is then I am hoping that this book has, in some way, changed your opinion. You could call it a life plan, a success strategy, your future objectives or you may decide to call it 'your life'. For the purpose of this chapter I will call it 'a life plan'.

Let's recap on how a sentence plan is decided upon. Information is gathered and used to build a positive structure of support and rehabilitation for the individual as they work towards their release date. Your release date is the day you wake up and realize you are in a position to free yourself from any inhibitions that are preventing you from finding contentment in your life. Your rehabilitation will focus on your ability to take on any challenge and, even if you are not successful, still enjoy the experience and learn from it. Your support systems will be your self-discipline as you take control of given situations that you did not feel in control of in the past.

Designing your life plan

First you need to build a profile of yourself to date that identifies your strengths and weaknesses, worries and woes and what you want from your future. This should be an enjoyable exercise, not an arduous task. If it is an arduous task then 'lighten up'. You need to balance your information with both negative and positive experiences.

Ultimately, what you are looking to produce is a picture of your life to date together with a set of aspirations for yourself with specific dates when you want to achieve them. Be careful not to put yourself into a corner with your life plan. If you set unrealistic goals such as planning to be a millionaire next year then you could be doomed to failure and this may only serve to strengthen your already low self-esteem and return you to your prison.

You will note that in the prison system you can move up levels but you can also move down. It is easy to tell people to be positive and reward themselves as they tick achieved objectives off their life plan. However, I am suggesting you follow a sentence plan structure, which means you will be disciplined if you do not adhere to your life plan.

Why, you may ask, would you want to discipline yourself? Because you need a balanced life. Failure is a fantastic learning experience and recognizing this helps us turn a negative experience into a positive outcome. If a prisoner is involved in a fight they may lose privileges and be moved down a level, and if they continue to disobey the rules they will lose further privileges. They are not rejected and considered a failure because the idea is to rehabilitate beliefs in order to help the individual conform to society. If they learn from their mistakes and their behaviour and attitude improves, they will be rewarded with a move to a higher level and possible early release.

I have observed people who set themselves goals. Their philosophy appears to be to try to achieve a goal but if they do not achieve it they do not worry. They give up and try again next year. I am suggesting that you consider a life plan that allows for failure. Ultimately, you are conditioning your mind to respond in a positive manner, even when the situation appears negative.

Do not be a victim. Some people spend their lives disciplining themselves and are unable to reward their achievements. How would you know if you were one of these people? If you are not enjoying achieving the levels then you may be a victim, and so part of your life plan could be to address this negative behaviour.

I have mentioned that a sentence plan is drawn up based on the areas for improvement agreed upon with those involved with the prisoner's development and, of course, the prisoner. You may also wish to involve other people when designing your life plan because sometimes others know us better than we realize. You may be setting objectives that are not realistic or you may be setting objectives that will not challenge you, preventing you from recognizing your true potential. I have drawn up three levels for you to achieve before starting on your life plan, which I believe will help you to focus on the task ahead.

- Basic: Life is not going to plan.

- Standard: Just another day.

- Enhanced: I have a lot to be grateful for.

- Premier: I have contentment in my life.

Here are the levels and the time-scales when you should review your progress, you will start on Basic.

- On Basic you will achieve the suggested objectives in the time allocated.

- You will remain on Basic until you have met all the objectives in the time specified.

- If you have achieved all your objectives on Basic you will move up to the next level.

- These rules will apply to each and every level.

- Your ultimate goal is to meet all the objectives on Enhanced level.

- Once you have met all the objectives on the Enhanced level in the set time, you will be free to write your own objectives for the Premier level.

You will note I have not detailed a Premier level. That is for you to do and this will be your life plan. To help you design your own Premier level, look back at the information you have collated.

Working from Basic to Premier level should help to discipline your behaviour. No one is perfect, so if you have to go down a level don't be too hard on yourself. This action should help you cope with disappointments in your life and teach you the skill of remaining positive as you assess the situation and bounce back to where you want to be in your life plan.

BASIC
You have 1 week to achieve the following:

Greet someone you have never greeted before.

Give someone a compliment.

Compliment yourself on a task well done.

Learn a new task.

Be aware of expressing positive body language.

Do not get upset over a failure.

Tidy up your room, garden, house or office.

Identify and analyse a negative experience.

Do some physical exercise. (See Chapter 11)

Eat a sensible diet. (See Chapter 12)

Make the effort to smile.

STANDARD
You have 4 weeks to achieve the following:

Do someone a big favour.

Contact someone you have not contacted in a long time.

Complete a task you have been meaning to do for months.

Listen, only, to someone's concerns.

Take to the charity shop any old clothes or items you have harboured for some time.

Buy yourself a present.

Raise a concern with someone in authority.

Turn a negative experience into a positive one.

Do some physical exercise. (See Chapter 11)

Eat a sensible diet. (See Chapter 12)

Make someone laugh.

ENHANCED
You have 3 months to achieve the following:
Raise some money for a charity.
Arrange a night out/a party.
Do an energetic activity you have never done before.
Learn a new skill.
Achieve a certificate.
Join some form of group, in a subject you are interested in.
Address a serious concern from your past.
Recognize only the positives in your daily life for one month.
Do some physical exercise. (See Chapter 11)
Eat a sensible diet. (See Chapter 12)
Make a group of people laugh.

PREMIER
You have 6 months to achieve the following:
It's now your turn to design the life plan you most want and recognize it.

Oliver: Fraud – three years

When Oliver left prison he took my advice and formulated a picture of his life to date together with a set of aspirations for himself. He set about achieving the Basic, Standard and Enhanced levels I had produced. He admitted things did not always go to plan and it took him approximately six months to complete all levels. Based on the aspirations he had identified for himself he drew up his Premier life plan.

He addressed the requirements as follows:

BASIC
You have one week to achieve the following:
Greet someone you have never greeted before.   *Oliver greeted his neighbour who he said annoys him.*
Give someone a compliment.   *Oliver complimented his probation officer by saying that she had helped him greatly. (He reported that she was so surprised she nearly fainted!)*
Compliment yourself on a task well done.   *Oliver complimented himself after he threw away his old address book with the names and numbers of his old partners in crime.*
Learn a new task.   *Oliver learnt to iron.*
Be aware of expressing positive body language.   *Oliver said he walked with his head held high.*
Do not get upset over a failure.   *Oliver did not get upset when he could not find the benefits office; he simply went home and called the helpline.*
Tidy up your room, garden, house or office.   *Oliver hoovered for the first time in years.*
Identify and analyse a negative experience.   *Oliver discovered the benefits office had moved. He had not read the address on the letter, so it was his fault he could not find it and he accepted responsibility.*
Do some physical exercise.   *Oliver said he walked and walked and enjoyed the freedom of being able to do so.*
Eat a sensible diet.   *Oliver avoided junk food.*
Make the effort to smile.   *Oliver said he had not stopped smiling since he left prison.*

STANDARD
You have 4 weeks to achieve the following:

Do someone a big favour.

While in prison Oliver had been part of the gardening team and so he used his new skills to tidy the garden of a disabled neighbour.

Contact someone you have not contacted in a long time.

Oliver contacted an uncle he had been close to as a child and set up a meeting to try to help him identify when his life had taken a turn for the worse.

Complete a task you have been meaning to do for months.

Oliver started looking for a full-time job. He signed up with various agencies, completed numerous application forms and secured a couple of interviews.

Listen, only, to someone's concerns.

Oliver listened to the concerns of his sister who was single with two kids and struggling to cope.

Take to the charity shop any old clothes or items you have harboured for some time.

Oliver had no problem with this task because he believed his entire wardrobe had become dated while he had been inside.

Buy yourself a present.

Oliver bought himself an alarm clock for his new job.

Raise a concern with someone in authority.

Oliver arranged a meeting with the employment office to discuss his concerns that his previous sentence could make finding a job difficult, and also to find out what support they could offer him.

Turn a negative experience into a positive one.

Oliver offered to give talks at the local youth clubs about the reality of prison life.

Do some physical exercise.

Oliver could not afford to join a gym and so he used library books to design his own keep-fit regime.

Eat a sensible diet.

Oliver sought advice from his local dietician and started on a low-fat diet.

Make someone laugh.

Oliver said he made himself laugh everyday he woke up and realized he was no longer in prison.

ENHANCED
You have 3 months to achieve the following:

Raise some money for a charity.

Oliver collected bric-a-brac from family and friends, sold it at a car boot sale and donated the money.

Arrange a night out/a party.

Oliver held a surprise birthday party for his wife.

Do an energetic activity you have never done before.

Oliver flew in a hot-air balloon.

Learn a new skill.

Oliver taught himself new gardening skills from books and worked on his own garden.

Achieve a certificate.

Oliver completed a CLAIT (Computer Literacy and Information Technology) course.

Join some form of group, in a subject you are interested in.

Oliver learnt to tango.

Address a serious concern from your past.

Oliver took ownership of his criminal past, he talked to a counsellor about his emotional guilt, he showed remorse.

Recognize only the positives in your daily life for one month.

Oliver kept a diary for a month which highlighted the positive aspects of each day.

Do some physical exercise.

Oliver continued with his exercise regime.

Eat a sensible diet.

Oliver began to appreciate the joys of cooking healthy balanced meals.

Make a group of people laugh.

Oliver organized a series of activities at his wife's birthday party that ensured everyone had a good laugh.

Oliver drew up and addressed the following Premier level.

PREMIER **You have 6 months to achieve the following:**
Secure full-time employment. *Oliver began working on a fruit and vegetable market stall.*
Make my boys proud of me. *Oliver regularly watched his two sons play football at weekends and joined his sons' coaching team.*
Save some money. *Oliver took a part-time job in his local pub and he saved all his earnings.*
Have a holiday. *Oliver took his wife and two children to Spain. This was the first time they had ever been abroad.*
Keep out of trouble. *Oliver distanced himself from his old friends and kept himself busy with his work and family.*
Look forwards with my life not backwards. *Oliver stopped looking for barriers in his life and concentrated on recognizing his life plan.*
Learn to love myself. *Oliver renewed his marriage vows. He believed he needed to learn to show others love, before he could love himself.*
Eat a healthy diet. *Working on the fruit and vegetable stall helped Oliver maintain a healthy diet.*
Exercise regularly. *Working on the coaching team kept Oliver fit.*
Keep to my life plan. *Oliver did it.*

Oliver did not re-offend. After a couple of years on the vegetable stall he started his own market stall selling vacuum-cleaner parts and continued to support his family in their new home. He continued to draw up a new life plan each year, and this was useful for me when I was putting this book together, as he kindly allowed me to use his life plan as an example. To date he has not felt the need to lower his level.

It is my belief that as you learn to appreciate the importance of your maturity and practise it in all aspects of your life, you will learn to be a far more contented individual. Maturity will also allow you to deal with situations you may have struggled with in the past.

I did not write this book for you to read once. You may need to read it a few times until its contents become part of your everyday thought process. Remember, you are the most important person in your life. Do not forget the violin player: practise, practise, practise.

I started this book talking about men in prison who cry for a variety of reasons. This was not to suggest that men in prison do not laugh – they do. I have arrived home from a session in a prison still laughing and I have numerous hilarious anecdotes that prisoners have told me that could fill a book. However, the laughter of a prisoner is never as genuine, pure, loud or jovial as that of a free man.

R U listenin'?

- As you advance through the levels you will be rewarded with a healthy self-esteem.

- Learn from your failures – do not stew on them.

- Appreciate the fact that you are in control.

- Dedication and discipline are key to your success.

- The tougher the task, the greater the reward.

- Start your life plan today! Remember, tomorrow never comes.

Chapter 15
Exercise Regime

 This chapter contains a selection of exercises linked to specific chapters. However, I would encourage you to develop these exercises to suit your learners' needs and use them as you deem appropriate.

I am not able to take credit for the design of all the following exercises. Some have always been around and I have no idea of their origins, while others have been adapted from training materials I have acquired along the way. What I can do, however, is vouch for their credibility. These are exercises I have used time and time again with positive outcomes. The majority are group exercises but there are some that can be done by individuals. I strongly recommend referring to them as exercises when working with groups. Using the word 'game' risks trivializing both the exercise and the outcome, allowing for such comments as, 'It's only a game.' – which could not be further from the truth.

I introduce the exercises early on in each chapter because if you use them early in a session this puts a smile on people's faces, relaxes them and starts their journey of self-discovery. When you achieve this it allows you the opportunity to work through the rest of the chapter identifying areas of concern everyone feels comfortable enough to address. In turn, this allows you to understand the needs of your group and work with them to come up with alternative methods for dealing with life's worries and woes that may have prevented them from recognizing their full potential.

The following are some pointers to bear in mind when delivering the exercises.

R U listenin'?

- Ensure your materials are relevant to your learners and adapt them where necessary.

- It is essential for the facilitator to read the whole chapter and ensure they have a grasp of its contents, before delivering the chapter as a session.

- On completion of each exercise you must take time to discuss the exercise and how individuals related to it. Not to do so, would make the exercise irrelevant.

- Be sure to present your materials in their best possible light, no scraps of paper or chewed pens. Use clean, well-presented handouts and resources.

- Well-ventilated rooms, plenty of space, light and water are all commonsensical issues that need to be considered.

- Identify any learning needs individuals may have before launching into a session.

- Be aware of your audience. Ask everyone to give a quick synopsis of their background and their expectations from the session. I occasionally have people in my groups who are experts in their field and I am careful not to make sweeping statements that may allow them to take me to task.

- Always give set times to complete tasks as this will keep your sessions on target and should keep everyone active.

- Remember there is no such thing as a wrong answer; any answer implies you are engaging with your learners, which is the aim of the exercise.

- As a facilitator you are responsible for painting the scene for any scenario or predicament. Having the ability to paint a picture in the minds of others is crucial for a genuine response. This is best achieved by covering the five senses when relating any of the above. If I am relaying a predicament I have found myself in, or a scenario I wish others to place themselves in, I will describe what I could see, hear, smell, taste and touch.

Enjoy the following exercises and remember you will only be taken as seriously as you take yourself.

GENERIC EXERCISE: CONCENTRATION

This can be used to focus the group's attention before any of the following exercises.

Aim:

To prove that, for some people, it's not the lack of ability to learn but possibly the lack of concentration that's holding them back.

Objective:

Learners will participate in a verbal and visual concentration exercise.

Exercise:

Inform everyone that you wish them to participate in a verbal and visual exercise. They are to be sent to prison and they must choose one item they would like to take with them. Everything will be allowed, provided you, as the facilitator or governor, give permission.

To receive permission the learners must introduce themselves ('My name is Bob.'), tell you where they are going ('I am going to prison.'), ask for permission to take a specific item ('Governor, can I please take') and name the item ('my CD collection?'). To receive permission they must request an item that begins with the same first letter as their first name (so Bob's request for CDs would be refused). In turn, give everyone an opportunity to ask for permission. Run the exercise until everyone has worked out the answer or you feel it is time to put people out of their misery.

Now switch to a visual exercise without informing the group. This time they are leaving prison and may go to any city, town or country in the world they wish. Again they will require the governor's permission. This time to receive permission, their (own) hands must be touching each other when they make their request.

Examples:

Verbal exercise: 'My name is Terry, I am going to prison and I would like permission to take my teddy bear.' 'Permission granted.' Visual exercise: 'My name is Terry, I would like permission to go to Liverpool.' (said with hands touching) 'Permission granted.'

Comments:

Were people concentrating at the beginning of the session when you clearly asked them to participate in a visual and verbal exercise? Did they get frustrated trying to give a verbal answer to the second exercise?

It will be useful to explain in your introduction that most people have a concentration span of approximately twenty minutes before their minds drift off. Momentarily, they may start thinking about (talking to themselves about) what's for dinner, what's on television that night, do they need to insure the car, whatever. Their minds will usually drift back to the matter in hand. This cannot be said for everyone. Some people have a concentration span of two minutes and once their mind wanders off a subject it never returns. Their self-talk may be causing their minds to wander as they involve themselves in a personal conversation. This exercise should enforce their need to concentrate for the duration of the session.

EXERCISE 1: PRISON LIFE (SEE CHAPTER 1)

Use with:

Groups.

Aim:

To make everyone appreciate the difficulties encountered when designing a prison that will serve as a place for punishment and rehabilitation.

Objective:

Using role-play, the group, working to a budget, will design a prison.

Exercise:

Design a prison using a list of buildings provided below. The brief is to take an A1 piece of paper and to draw a horizontal and vertical line representing the corridors linking prison wings. At each point where the lines touch the edge of the paper, they are to draw a square representing a wing where the prisoners are housed. See diagram below.

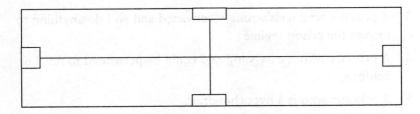

Using the list below, write the names of the buildings and their costs on separate pieces of card. Place all the cards onto the prison design; extra corridors linking the facilities may be added.

Buildings for prison design:

Swimming pool £50,000	Cinema/bowling alley £75,000	IT suite/library £50,000
Fast-food bar £50,000	Gym £50,000	All-weather football pitch £75,000
Golf course £50,000	Mechanical workshop £25,000	Bar £50,000
Construction workshop £75,000	Education block £75,000	Music studio £25,000
Health spa £50,000	Dentist's surgery £25,000	Doctor's surgery £25,000
Amusement arcade £25,000	Psychologist £25,000	Segregation block £50,000
Staff mess/bar £50,000	Chapel £25,000	Prison kitchen £75,000

Using the role-play characters below, write each character on a separate strip of card and distribute them, one each. Then inform the group of the Home Office's decision to cut their budget to £500,000. The dilemma is what facilities to remove from their design to meet the Home Office requirements.

Example: Role-play

1. A prisoner who has a wife and three children and is desperate to learn a trade to help him find work before he is released.

2. A prisoner with no qualifications and is desperate to achieve something before leaving prison.

3. A prisoner who feels wrongly convicted and will do anything to disrupt the prison regime.

4. A prisoner who is easygoing and could be persuaded to rebel or conform.

5. A prisoner who is a hypochondriac.

6. A prisoner serving a life sentence.

7. A prisoner who refuses any form of education.

8. A teacher who believes education is crucial in a prison.

9. A probation officer who believes prisons should be more relaxed.

10. A nurse who is concerned about the prisoners' physical and mental health.

Comments:

Will the prisoners insist on a fun-filled prison with no responsibilities or will they accept the benefits of a more disciplined, educational environment? Do the staff have the skills to negotiate with the prisoners and make them realize they should use their time in prison constructively or will they end up with a holiday camp? Feel free to design your own buildings and characters.

Ultimately can your learners relate to the exercise, do they appreciate the need to lead a disciplined life or are they looking for the fun-filled life free from responsibilities?

EXERCISE 2: AN ACCESSORY TO THE CRIME (SEE CHAPTER 2)

Use with:

Groups.

Aim:

To help learners identify if they are self-harming (in the context of Chapter 2).

Objective:

For the group to participate in an auction and bid for self-harming behaviour they can relate to.

Exercise:

The facilitator, using an A1 flipchart, draws up a list with suggestions from the whole group, of the ten most common self-harming attributes people display.

Each learner is then given £100 in denominations of £5. They are told to bid for any of the self-harming attributes they can relate to. Bids can only be at the rate of £5; large bids of £50 spoil the dynamics and fun of the auction.

The facilitator begins the auction. Each time an attribute is purchased the facilitator takes the money and writes the person's name and bid against the purchase. This continues until all the attributes have been auctioned.

Example:

Here are some self-harming attributes to prompt your group:

- Talking yourself down.

- Not taking regular exercise.

- Eating and drinking too much.

- Getting angry with others.

- Feeling lethargic.

- Wallowing in self-pity.

- Feeling lonely.

- Not eating healthy food.

- Worrying.

- Wasting valuable time.

Comments:

On completion of the exercise, explain how their purchase, or attempted purchase, of particular attributes displays how much the negative attributes are impacting on their life. They now need to consider how they will address their self-harming behaviour. Further reading of this chapter will offer insight and ideas.

EXERCISE 3: BELIEVING YOUR WAY OUT FROM WITHIN (SEE CHAPTER 3)

Use with:

Groups or individuals.

Aim:

To appreciate that if the reward is great enough we can motivate ourselves to achieve.

Objective:

Learners will identify a goal they wish to achieve and the motivating factor that would make them achieve it.

Exercise:

Have everyone think of a goal they would like to achieve but do not feel capable of doing so. Produce a one-million pound note (that you have made), ask your students to enter into your belief that this is a real one-million pound note. Now ask them if they would be able to achieve their goal, if the reward was the million pound note. Remember to stress what they could do with the money: new house, car, holiday; the answer is usually 'yes'.

Example:

Goals: Achieve a GCSE, lose weight.

Comments:

For obvious reasons the goal cannot be, for example, a woman aged 25, growing 2 cm taller or a bald man growing his hair back.

EXERCISE 4: KNOWING YOUR SENTENCE (SEE CHAPTER 4)

Use with:

Groups or individuals.

Aim:

To identify the roots of specific beliefs and change them if desired.

Objective:

To explore how personal beliefs can impact on the way we lead our lives.

Exercise:

Have your learners write five words or a sentence expressing how they would describe themselves, and then get them to write five words or a sentence illustrating how they perceive other people view them. What they are doing is drawing up their beliefs. Ask them to analyse their statements and see if they are negative or positive. Often they tend to be negative. Ask them to take a belief they do not like about themselves and begin working on changing it.

Get them to speak to people who know them well and ask them why they think they have a particular belief (this exercise may be done over more than one session). This can offer them the valuable information they need to address their belief. Most important is to recognize how destructive beliefs can be, and that they may have been hiding behind their belief as a way of justifying their lifestyle (i.e. the person who believes they are lazy will lead the lifestyle of a lazy person).

Examples:

The following statements are from people who have come back to me having talked to others regarding their beliefs.

- I was surprised how insignificantly other people view what I consider to be a serious failing in my personality.

- Talking to older family members offered me a great insight into where my beliefs stemmed from.

- I was amazed how many people have the same beliefs or concerns that I have.

- I was offered the solution to my concern and it was so simple, I had just been ignoring it all my life.

- Talking about my beliefs with others, rather than keeping them to myself, was a breath of fresh air.

- Others were quickly able to contradict my negative beliefs with positive ones.

- It made me realize there are no prizes for holding on to negative beliefs.

- I acknowledge that I have been using my negative beliefs to justify my lifestyle.

Comments:

Most people find that beliefs come from a person or a situation that was important to them. Discussing their beliefs with others who may have similar concerns, will offer them the support needed to working through negative beliefs.

EXERCISE 5: NATURAL INSTINCTS (SEE CHAPTER 5)
Use with:

Groups or individuals.

Aim:

Understand the need to be proactive in relationships, if we want to maintain and strengthen them.

Objective:

To identify genetically related people in the lives of your learners who are important and suggest ways in which they can maintain a closer contact, if they wish to do so.

Exercise:

Everyone is given a piece of A4 paper on which they draw a square in the centre, big enough for them to write their name in. Inform your learners that the square represents a prison they have placed themselves in. They are now to think of five genetically related people in their lives they would miss most if they were in a real prison. Next, have them randomly write the names of the people they have thought of on the piece of paper, spread the names around the page but not next to each other. Now, have them draw a line between the person's name and the square containing their name. The closer they are to the person, the shorter the line should appear.

Pose the following question: 'In one year, would you like to see your line remain the same length, be reduced or lengthened?' If the answer is reduced, how are they going to do it?

Example:

I wish the line to my mother were shorter. Solution: make the effort to tell her that you love her, visit her more often, take flowers, phone her every week, send her letters, tell her how much she means to you.

Comments:

If someone puts a person's name on their piece of paper but insists the person they have identified is not really that important to them, in my experience this is not so. If the person were not important to them they would not have thought of them in the first instance. Point out that they may be in denial about their feelings towards this person. Ask them to consider the benefits of reducing the length of the line to the person. Understanding their relationship with this person could be of greater benefit to them than reducing the length of the line, which may indicate a good relationship in the first instance.

EXERCISE 6: OFFENDING BEHAVIOUR (SEE CHAPTER 6)

Use with:

Groups.

Aim:

To prove that all their needs can be addressed. It's the level at which the need can be realistically addressed that often acts as a barrier.

Objective:

For the group to detail specific needs in their lives and identify how they can meet their needs, now.

Exercise:

Ask your learners to think of a famous person they would like to be for a day and then ask them to write down three reasons why they would like to be this person. For example, if someone chooses David Beckham their three reasons might be: 1. Money, 2. Plays football, 3. Good physique. Explain how their reasons can be seen as needs and that their needs can be met, although not at the same level as David Beckham.

Example:

1. The need for money. Solution: get a job. 2. The need to play football. Solution: join a local team. 3. The need for a good physique. Solution: get down the gym and work out. The reasons will often fit into Maslow's hierarchy of needs, which is discussed in some detail in Chapter 6.

Comments:

Learners usually think this is a trick question and say they are happy being themselves. Before you start the exercise explain it is not a trick question. They will need to think of a famous person, for the exercise to be of benefit.

EXERCISE 7: SEGREGATION (SEE CHAPTER 7)

Use with:

Groups.

Aim:

To increase self-awareness and an understanding of personality traits people accept or reject.

Objective:

Participate in a group activity to understand how others react to individual behaviour patterns.

Exercise:

Ask your learners to place an elasticized headband around their head, using a selection of cards with personality traits written on them (i.e. bully, joker, miserable, generous). Have them place a card in their headband without looking at it. The aim of the exercise is for them in turn to guess what is written on their card. The group discuss the following scenario: they have each been given a custodial sentence but are in the unique position of being able to choose their cellmate. Working clockwise around the group and without mentioning what is written on anyone's card, the qualities of each member are discussed based on their card. At the end of the discussion, again clockwise, each member is informed by the rest of the group if they would be prepared to share a cell with them, offering reasons why they would or would not like to share. The individual then guesses what is written on their card.

Example:

John has 'bully' written on his card, the group will discuss the positive and negative benefits of sharing a cell with him and decide if they would like to share with him.

Comments:

If the learner fails to guess what is on their card this could display a lack of self-awareness and a misunderstanding of personality traits accepted or rejected by others. This should not be seen as a negative outcome but positive. The learner may have identified why they have not been successful in areas of their life (i.e. making lasting relationships, getting a job, experiencing contentment) and now know what they have to work on.

EXERCISE 8: INSTITUTIONALIZATION (SEE CHAPTER 8)
Use with:

Groups.

Aim:

The learner should understand which they prefer: being told what to do (institutionalization) or making decisions for themselves (independence).

Objective:

To make and throw two paper aeroplanes to a set marker. The first aeroplane is made and thrown under instruction the second is under their own steam.

Exercise:

The facilitator will be instructing the group for the first part of the exercise. Under instruction they will be expected to make a paper aeroplane from a set of instructions and throw it to a set marker on the floor. If the plane does not reach its marker or flies past it, they will be told by the facilitator to adjust the plane or move the marker to a position where they now know the plane can fly to. When the facilitator is satisfied that the requirements of the exercise have been met, their part in the exercise is complete.

For the second part of the exercise, the learner will repeat the exercise without instruction. They will be responsible for the making of the plane, the predicted flying distance and any amendments to the plane or flying distance they believe necessary to achieve the objective.

Example:

For the first instructed part of the exercise, I usually take a paper plane-making example off the Internet. Use an example that fits an A4 piece of paper detailing the fold lines the learner needs to follow and a clear set of instructions you can read aloud. Try making the plane yourself before the exercise to ensure it is 'do-able' and not too complicated.

I use an A1 flipchart as a scoreboard, on which I note predicted flying distance, actual flying distance, attempts, achievements and failures.

Comments:

It is important that planes are not thrown until instructed to do so; I find that I have to stress this before starting the exercise.

EXERCISE 9: REHABILITATION (SEE CHAPTER 9)

Use with:

Groups or individuals.

Aim:

To appreciate that simply posing the question out loud, 'What have I got to do?' in a given situation allows the individual to take control of the situation and display independence.

Objective:

The learner will identify situations in their lives where they do not feel in control, using the question 'What have I got to do?' They will detail what they need to do in order to take control.

Exercise:

Split the group into two lines standing opposite each other. Have the people in one line give the person opposite them a personal item (i.e. watch, mobile phone, ring). Take the group who have received the item outside the room, instruct them that they are not to return the item to the owner until the owner has used the following sentence. 'What have I got to do to get my watch/ mobile phone/ring back?' Return them to the room, have them line up in the same positions and begin the exercise.

After completion of the exercise, have your learners consider what they want in their life at that particular moment in time. This could relate to short- or long-term goals. For example, it could be that they want more money and the only realistic way to achieve this is with a promotion, or by getting another job with better pay. They decide to arrange a meeting with their boss to discuss the possibility of promotion. The key words for them to remember in the conversation are, 'What have I got to do?' because this question allows them to take control of the situation, gives them a specific goal to aim for and places a commitment on the other person. They ask their boss what they need to do in order to earn a promotion and the reply is, 'They need to meet all the targets he has set for them.' They are now in a position to take control of their destiny and recognize their promotion because they know what they need to do.

Example:

Other occasions when you can use this statement are:

What have I got to do to buy a new car?

What have I got to do to lose weight?

What have I got to do to improve my computer skills?

What have I got to do to be independent?

Comments:

As always, the learner must be realistic in the first instance about the situation they wish to take control of.

EXERCISE 10: KNOW YOUR JAILERS (SEE CHAPTER 10)

Use with:

Groups.

Aim:

To appreciate the benefits of a structured lifestyle.

Objectives:

Learners will draw up their own time-management planner.

Exercise:

Monitor your time for one week. Detail every hour by filling in a 24-hour time-table. Add up the total for leisure, work and sleep. This will give you an idea of how you are balancing your week and will highlight where the majority of your hours are utilized. Your sleep time should be between 50 and 60 hours, working time between 35 and 40 hours and the remaining time should be divided between leisure and other activities.

STEP 1

- If you do not have a nice watch – buy one – respect time.

- Write goals that you can action today on a daily 'to do' list.

- Short-term goals can be built into a monthly diary.

- Long-term goals should be written on a wall-chart calendar for the year. (This will act as a constant visual reminder of the dates when your goals should be achieved.)

- Monitor when you are happy to address the majority of your daily duties and this will help you recognize when you are most productive in your day.

STEP 2

- Write down all the tasks you need to do.

- Categorize them into three columns as in the diagram below:

COLUMN 1 URGENT	COLUMN 2 IMPORTANT	COLUMN 3 BENEFICIAL
A meeting A one-day sale	Doctor's appointment Helping a friend move home	Attending the gym Going to a lecture

STEP 3

You should be able to build any goals you wish to achieve into your time-management plan. However, do not force yourself into a 'no win' situation, e.g. 'I want to pass my driving test before I am 21.' This is too specific and you are setting yourself up to fail. If you fail, there is a chance you will not bother trying again. However, 'I want to have 20 lessons and take my driving test before I am 21,' is achievable. If you are not successful you can address your time-management planner and try again.

STEP 4

Your plan should allow for unforeseen emergencies and crises in life. If you are not achieving your targets it could be that you are being too ambitious, or you have not allocated your tasks appropriately. Remember, urgent matters should be addressed when you are most productive and for many people this is first thing in the morning. Non-urgent matters should be kept for when you are not so productive and this, for many people, is the evening. You should feel comfortable with your time-management plan, not driven by the thought of failure, but optimistic about the pleasure of achievement.

STEP 5

Your leisure time is a reward; do not sacrifice it because you have not achieved a goal. Be honest with your assessment of why you have not recognized a goal. Restructure your time-management planner to ensure this does not happen again and learn from your mistakes. Do not try to play catch-up using your leisure time.

STEP 6

Everyone's time-management planner is different. What is a priority to you is a necessity to someone else, and your 'peak time' in a day will be a 'rest time' for another person. You may prefer to work in large chunks of time while others like to work in short spurts.

Example:

I am worried about finishing this book on time for my publisher. I build into my planner 30 minutes a day for extra writing time in the morning when I know I am at my peak. I make an appointment with my publisher to discuss my concerns and arrange a meeting with people I know, who are writing a book, to share good practice.

Comments:

I suggest you set aside or 'book' time in your planner for worrying. Worrying is part of our survival and is a valuable tool in self-discipline. Anyone who does not worry is probably from another planet! Without worry we would not pay our gas bills on time, keep an eye on a boiling pan or turn up for work on time each day. However, there is a time and place for everything. Put a couple of dates in your weekly timetable to worry, say 6.30–7.00 pm Tuesday and Thursday. Detail the worries you have and build them into your overall planner. I am not suggesting for a moment that you sit and worry for half an hour but rather that you look at your worries and think of ways of tackling them.

EXERCISE 11: THE GYM (SEE CHAPTER 11)

Use with:

Groups.

Aim:

To appreciate that exercise is fun – it's all about discovering the right exercise for you.

Objective:

To create and participate in a physically active exercise.

Exercise:

This exercise calls for space. If you are working in a training room you will need to move all the furniture to the edge of the room. If you are fortunate enough to be able to access a gymnasium, or take your group out into an open area where you can set up a badminton net or similar apparatus, then do so.

    Let's assume we are in a training room situation, with all the furniture at the edge of the room to create as much space as possible. Hang a length of rope across the centre of the room. Ask two volunteers to stand either side of the line. Introduce a medium-sized child's (soft) ball. The volunteers are required to hit the ball to each other over the rope. Other learners are encouraged to join in, but before they join in, they must introduce a new rule to the exercise. Once they have introduced the rule, they join alternating sides and are responsible for ensuring everyone obeys their new rule. If you wish, you may introduce a 'sin bin', where people not following a ruling will be sent for a one-minute time penalty before rejoining the exercise.

Example:

The first person to join states you can only hit the ball over the rope with your hand. The next person suggests you can use your head as well. The next suggests you must call out your name before hitting the ball, the next person states that two people on your side of the rope must hit the ball before it goes back over the rope, and so on.

Comments:

This is an energetic exercise; appropriate clothing will need to be considered before suggesting the exercise. Overall it should be great fun and the stamina of your learners will determine the length of the exercise. Finish by having your group draw up a list of physical activities they would enjoy, i.e., outward-bound activities, trying a new sport at the local leisure centre, a sport they may have played in the past such as a water sport, walking, dancing; anything that involves physical exercise. Then encourage them to be proactive and engage in their suggestions.

EXERCISE 12: KITCHENS (SEE CHAPTER 12)

Use with:

Groups or individuals.

Aim:

For the group to understand what foods are best for their well-being.

Objectives:

For the group to complete a food quiz.

Exercise:

QUESTIONS

1. What are the five main nutrients?
2. What is the function of enzymes?
3. Which of the following can be affected by the food we eat?

    o Anxiety
    o Panic attacks
    o Cravings or food addictions
    o Depression
    o Aggression
    o Impaired memory
    o Insomnia

4. What does GDA stand for?
5. What is the daily calorie intake for a male?
6. What is the daily calorie intake for a female?
7. Fill in the missing words:

    (a) Fibre: Keeps you _____.
    (b) Protein: Important for growth and _____ the body.
    (c) Salt: Beware, too much will give you _____ blood
        pressure, possible stomach cancer and can lead to kidney
        failure, but you do need some.
    (d) Vitamins: Help cells _____ normally.
    (e) Minerals: We require a variety of minerals. They supplement
        the body in numerous ways including the _____, bones,
        teeth, and cells.
    (f) Carbohydrates: Give us _____.
    (g) Fats: Are a good source of energy. They help us to absorb some
        vitamins and contain important things called essential
        _____ _____.

8. How many glasses of water should you drink in a day?

9. True or false: The most important liquid for a healthy body and mind is water.

10. Dehydration can sometimes be mistaken for_____

_____.

ANSWERS

1. Carbohydrates, protein, fat, vitamins and fibre.

2. Enzymes break down the swallowed food into liquid from which the digested nutrients are absorbed and carried into the bloodstream to the parts of the body where they are needed.

3. All of the above are affected by the food we eat.

4. Guideline Daily Amounts.

5. 2500.

6. 2000.

7. (a) Regular.

(b) Healing.

(c) High.

(d) Reproduce.

(e) Blood.

(f) Energy.

(g) Fatty acids.

8. 6 to 8.

9. True.

10. Hunger pangs.

Example:

I use photos to answer the questions; I believe it helps the learners focus.

Comments:

To give your group a fighting chance, you may want to hand out the quiz in advance of your session.

EXERCISE 13: FREEDOM (SEE CHAPTER 13)

Use with:

Groups.

Aim:

To prove to your learners they have the maturity necessary to deal with a variety of dilemmas in their lives.

Objective:

The group will offer advice on a variety of uncomfortable dilemmas.

Exercise:

Write a variety of dilemmas on cards, some for fun, others more serious and relevant to this chapter. Distribute the cards, one to each learner. Have them in turn read their card aloud, then ask the rest of the group individually to offer advice.

Example:

DILEMMAS:

1. I think I might be gay.

2. I am so lonely.

3. I have no academic qualifications, which makes me dumb.

Possible advice offered:

1. I have a gay friend who is very happy. There are gay helplines if you want to speak to someone. It's not a bad thing being gay.

2. Visit your local library, find out what groups meet locally that might be of interest. Look at some credible websites to identify a new sport or hobby. Speak to your doctor.

3. There are evening classes available if you want to gain qualifications. Speak to your boss, some companies will help you to improve your education. Make an appointment to speak to a careers advisor.

Comments:

What you have done with this exercise is prove to your learners they have the maturity to think through difficult dilemmas and resolve them.

Bibliography

Bond, T. (1986) *Games for Social and Life Skills*. London: Hutchinson Education.

Food Standards Agency (1995) *Manual of Nutrition*, 10th edn, Ed. by J. Woolfe. London: HMSO.

Maslow, A.H. (1987) *Motivation and Personality*, 3rd edn, Rev. by R. Frager, J. Fadiman, C. McReynolds, R. Cox. New York: HarperCollins.

Morris, N. and Rothman, D.J. (eds) (1995) *The Oxford History of the Prison: The Practice of Punishment in Western Society*. Oxford and New York: Oxford University Press.

Useful websites

www.nhsdirect.nhs.uk/encyclopaedia/a-z Not being an expert on health, this website was good for referencing all aspects of health and diet in easy-to-read chunks.

www.hmprisonservice.gov.uk This website offers more information on, and insight into the running of the prison service than one might expect. I used the website to affirm my understanding of prison procedures.

www.news.bbc.co.uk I used this website to reference and cross-reference a host of subjects. It is easy to navigate and offers reliable information.

www.mind.org.uk I like the way Mind take a holistic approach to the Cause of Mental Health. The website helped me check my understanding of mental health in a positive light.